MW00893177

LIFE
LESSONS

(Don't Learn Them Late!)

FRED WITT

Fred Witt is the author of:

Things I Wish I Knew:
A Compendium of Lessons Learned Late

Copyright © 2010 Fred Witt
All Rights Reserved

ISBN: 1449985831
ISBN-13: 9781449985837

www.fredwitt.com

To my three gifts, Aaron, Tyler and Olivia
You inspire me more

CONTENTS

PREFACE   ix

PART I: FOUNDATION   1

  1. The Story of Icarus   3

  2. Best Investment   9

  3. Goals   19

  4. Persistence   27

  5. Decisions, Decisions   31

  6. Biggest Decision   35

  7. Adaptability   39

PART II: BUILDING YOUR BRAND   43

  8. It's About People, Not Money   45

  9. Mentors: Everything's Been Done Before   49

  10. Learn To   55

  11. Accountability   79

PART III: PARADIGMS SHIFT: PARADOXES APPEAR   83

   12. What Motivates You   85

   13. Cognitive Dissonance   89

   14. Ethics   95

   15. Preparation   99

   16. Age Thirty-Five   105

   17. Random Thoughts   109

   18. The Meaning of Life   119

PART IV: FOUR WORDS   123

   19. Four Words For Your Journey   125

PART V: CONCLUSION   131

ENDNOTES   137

ACKNOWLEDGEMENTS   139

ABOUT THE AUTHOR   143

PREFACE

I wish life came with an instruction manual.

I recently purchased a new vacuum cleaner. Not exactly the most exciting event to report in one's life, but it had meaning. What struck me was the quality of advancing technology. I'm not referring to the machine itself, but to the instructions provided. It came with not one, but two different instruction books. One was written out in orderly detail on subjects ranging from "How To Turn On" to "Trouble Shooting." The second was even more impressive. It had *pictures*. Yes, the second document summarized the first and reduced everything I needed to know into two pages of pictures. I was excited because this, I could understand.

If they have instruction manuals for a vacuum cleaner, and every other machine created, why can't they have one for life? What if life's instruction manual had handy categories, such as "Operating" and "Trouble Shooting." Admit it – wouldn't your life be better if, in times of need, you could pull out your manual and trouble shoot your way out of … trouble?

In my dream of a better life, I imagine walking across the stage of my high school graduation (in Nebraska, no less) and receiving from the Principal both my high school diploma and a sturdy, hard cover book. Being an excited graduate, I wouldn't understand the significance at the moment (the joke, of course, is that you should hire a teenager while they still know everything), but I knew I should tuck the book away in a drawer to be pulled out in a time of need or simple curiosity. This book would be called something like "Life Lessons" and the byline would instruct "Don't Learn Them Late!" Evidencing seriousness, the letters would be embossed in gold. Inside, the book would offer simple lessons and advice about practical stuff you need to know. Stuff that, long ago, you were forced to learn quickly from Grandpa on the farm or an old boss in the factory. Stuff you're not formally taught in school, but need to know in order to function and operate in a complex work world. It's not necessarily knowledge, but wisdom about every day life, that should be imparted.

What are the rules, especially the unwritten ones, of the workplace? How should you interact with co-workers of different ages and positions of authority? How do you "roll with the punches" and understand that a lot of what goes on in the business world is "not about you?" How do you communicate and learn to appreciate that how you say something can be as important as what you say. Are there types of people that "should be avoided at all costs?" Isn't it simple, especially if we all work for the same company? Isn't everyone on the same team and isn't loyalty valued above all else? After all, life is fair and the situation is always equal isn't it? For example, if your company expects your undying loyalty, doesn't your company reward you with its' loyalty in return?

I wish I knew then what I know now. I was unprepared for the complexities of life and the complexities of the workplace. Worse, for me, I became a lawyer and was thrust into an adversarial environment. The "other side" wanted to run over me, and the more complete the victory, the better. I was confused the first time an opposing lawyer boasted that he was going to "clean my clock" (to put it mildly). What did either my clock or me have to do with us working as respected and respectful professionals on this matter? Do you see my problem? I was a one-dimensional thinker in a three dimensional world. Stated simply, I was clueless!

I learned many lessons the hard way. My life would've been so much better, and my career progressed in a more linear path upward, if a wise mentor pulled me aside and hit me over the head with my "Life Lessons" book. I desperately needed help understanding human nature and how things worked in the "real" business world. I also needed some gentle (or at times, not so gentle) reminders to stop "messing up." I needed a better grip on the big picture and my little role in it. I needed a fresh break from my dysfunctional past and a new start on my exciting future.

I'd get upset when things went wrong and I was easily knocked off balance. I'd let anybody or most anything affect me. It was like I was in a little boat in the middle of the rough, and endless, ocean of life. Calm seas were the exception and my little boat was constantly tossed around subject to the whims of the environment.

For whatever reason, I attracted a cast of characters that fed off my weaknesses for their own benefit. This, of course, fueled my insecurities and caused my stomach to churn. One day I realized something profound (at least for me). I didn't matter to "them," and unless I decided to take control over my life and my emotions, I would remain stuck in endless rough water. Basically, I had to decide that nothing could be done to me without my permission. The fewer who had my permission to "yank my chain," the more power I had over the situation. The calmer the emotions, the better I was at performing the difficult tasks at hand. Does this sound familiar to you? I'd guess that, at some point in your life, you've experienced the same emotional difficulties as me.

I'm convinced I could've handled the situations more effectively (and in a fraction of the time) if I had a "life" manual. I needed a guidebook that I could turn to in my many times of need. I wished I'd learned more about "big picture" items that the self-help or business books don't talk about. For example, there's a lot about life and human nature that's counter-intuitive. You'll find your old friends imploring you to "follow us." However, your great future (the one you've imagined) requires you to say "goodbye," choosing a different path that's long, lonely and difficult. You'll find situations in which, from your perspective, you think things are equal – only to discover that the stakes, motivations or agendas of others are dramatically different. Failing to appreciate human nature and the motivations of others can put your career in peril. Life is also filled with double standards and comments like "well, everybody does it." Understanding this is an excuse and not a reason, is helpful. Resolving in advance not to follow the crowd down the "wrong" path is imperative.

With a chuckle about the crazy path my life has taken, I'd like to share my thoughts on business life. I'm not an expert and I haven't done the research, but there are certain things my experience tells me are true. There are also many things I've learned late. I'd like to imagine I'm writing a book to be given to that bright-eyed eighteen-year-old who's excited about leaving home and taking on what the working world has to offer. A simple manual on how things work in the "real" world.

So, let's get started on that life manual, focusing on the things you need to know to prepare you for the "rough and tumble" of reality. My objective is to discuss many topics as briefly as possible. Less is the new more!

My one regret? I can't draw. Because, if I could, I can assure you this book would be filled with pictures. Better yet, anyone know how to write a pop-up book?

PART I: FOUNDATION

1. THE STORY OF ICARUS

With apologies to my English teachers and students of Greek Mythology, I'd like to imperfectly recount the story of Icarus.

Daedalus was exiled to an island. Although an escape by land and sea was not possible, Daedalus altered the natural order of things and invented wings to fly. His wings were made of feathers held together by bees' wax and were curved like the wings of a bird. He made two sets – one for him and one for his son, Icarus. When the wings were finished and they were ready to fly, his father warned Icarus about the dangers of flight and instructed him to fly only between the extremes. If he flew too low, the moisture would weigh his wings down and if he flew too high, the Sun would melt them. With his father in the lead, Icarus took flight. After beginning carefully and following his father's instructions, Icarus soon began to master the art of flight. With boyish excitement, and literally throwing caution to the wind, Icarus left his father and soared higher. Ultimately, flying too close to the Sun, his wings melted just as his father warned and he crashed into the sea.

Daedalus was one of the wisest men of his time. He wanted only the best for his son and he gave Icarus two of the most amazing gifts – his freedom and the gift of flight. Daedalus was the type of parent that went "above and beyond." He not only invented the means to fly but also personally instructed his son on how to fly. He did something remarkable – he gave his son the "instruction book," complete with "what to do" and, as important, "what not to do." He even added a warning label with clear and simple words.

Icarus had the easy part of the bargain. To be free and have a great life, indeed, have God-like powers, all Icarus had to do was listen to his father's advice and fly between the extremes – meaning, live life in moderation. His father had done all the hard work and the only thing he asked of Icarus was to follow directions. No need to think – just do what you're told. No need to worry – just be faithful.

I can imagine the flying lesson went something like this:

"Follow me, Icarus. Flying is dangerous, but you can do it if you carefully follow my directions."

"Flap your wings like this."

"Follow my example and do it just like me! Yes, Icarus, like that!"

"Yes, you can do it son! Way to go!"

"You're flying! You've got it!"

"Now, Icarus, all that's left is the easy part. Yeah, that's right – fly between the extremes – and stay away from the Sun!"

"Did you hear me, Icarus? Do you understand?"

"Icarus, you're going too high!"

"I'm warning you. Stay away from the Sun or your wings will melt!"

"No, Icarus, No!"

This is a story of a young boy who could not keep his ego and boyish exuberance in check and, doing the one thing his father warned him not to, Icarus paid the ultimate price. He not only squandered his gift, but he foolishly lost his life in the process. Even worse, his grief-stricken father witnessed the loss of his only son. A heroic story of human triumph followed by tragedy recounted in Greek mythology.

Does this story sound familiar to you? Does it still have relevance over two thousand years later? How is that possible? With the pace of our life changing by the minute, how can an ancient myth have any value today? The myth's relevant because it tells a story about the basic human condition that is constant. Times change, but people don't.

If they had newspapers back then, I'm sure the bold headline in the **Crete Island Gazette** would've read something like this:

"Given God-like Power of Flight, Icarus Falls to Death

Ignoring Warnings, He Flew Too Close to Sun

What Was He Thinking?"

There are some life lessons that are so important and so fundamental that they become critical building blocks for a successful life. If you can't learn them, or simply refuse to believe these lessons, you're in for a long and difficult life filled with disappointment. On the other hand, get these fundamental lessons right (even early), and you're off to a great start.

Do you feel life owes you something? Do you feel entitled? Do you insist on your own way without regard to the feelings of others? If your parents were to give you something, like new clothes, a car, tuition money, an inheritance or, like Icarus, your freedom to fly, how would you react? Would you be grateful for the gift and live modestly? Would you be thankful and live with humility? Would you appreciate that it wasn't your effort, toil and sacrifice that produced the gift? Would you share your good fortune with others? Would you realize you've been given a good start, but not a head start, and work even harder?

Or, like Icarus, would you defy your father and fly off without any respect for limits and boundaries? Would you act like it was you that invented the wings and there's no question "you know it all?" Would you act with undue pride and self-interest? Simply, would you let success go to your head? Oh, my.

What are some of the lessons to be learned? Well, starting with the obvious, because of life's experiences, our elders know more and deserve our respect? If a person in authority warns you not to do something, put your ego in check and listen? If your father asks you not to do something, make the easy choice and don't do it?

How about this simple one – it's not about you. There are forces and powers in the universe that are far beyond you and don't mess with them! A balanced ego is a good thing, but ego run amok is sure to lead to trouble? That small acts of teenage rebellion are part of the growing process, but continued acts of rebellion played out over a lifetime are sure to lead to misery? Who are you proving wrong and for what benefit?

Daedalus wanted his son to enjoy life, but live in moderation and follow a few simple rules – something every parent wishes for their child today. The problem is that God gave us Free Will and the power to choose. Ultimately, the decision is one we get to make daily, alone. It's up to us and we get to choose. No one can do it for us. That means you have the power to make great decisions with your ego in check. You can choose humility. This is great news! Why would you mess this one up?

Mark Twain had a wonderful perspective to offer on this topic: "When I was a boy of fourteen, my father was so ignorant I could hardly stand to have the old man around. But when I got to be twenty-one, I was astonished at how much the old man had learned in seven years!"

How will you know when you are "flying too close to the Sun?" When you're regularly ignoring the advice of your parents. When you're disrespecting others and acting in a selfish manner, always insisting on your own way. When you know you're doing things you shouldn't be doing at a time you shouldn't be doing them. When you're exhausted by the constant effort required to "swim against the stream." When your relationships are suffering. When your health is "out of whack" (I have no idea what a "whack" is). When you're getting too many of any of these: grades slipping, a loss of friends and/or running with the "wrong crowd," warnings at work, traffic tickets, little scrapes with the law, "close calls," addictive behaviors, outbursts of anger, etc. Well, you get the idea – it's too hot near the Sun!

Interestingly, the lessons provided by Icarus will also apply during your adult years. As you mature and your work environment gets more complex and dynamic, the signs will be less obvious. A person, who's alert and mindful of her environment, will easily spot them. One common situation is the tendency to be in a meeting and try, whether consciously or not, to be the "smartest person in the room." Invariably, there is one person in a business meeting who tries to dominate the conversation and be the one who has all the answers. Often, there's a rush to be the "smartest person in the room," and the duel will begin. I've been in a lot of meetings, and I've come to the conclusion that the smartest person in the room is seldom the one that talks a lot. A person that says the most, the loudest, seldom is the most intelligent or effective. In fact, it may be the opposite. The most intelligent person is likely the one listening and asking probing questions in order to understand. The person speaking a little, and last. Remember, don't be an Icarus! Live with humility as your guidepost, and listening to others as your habit.

There's no question humility and listening will be a challenge in your life. After all, we're human and it's difficult to live life in balance. It's difficult to control our ego. It's not easy to live with humility as your guidepost, especially when you're set free and experience success. There'll be many times in your life when you'll feel like you've "known it all" or "done it all." There's no question you'll need help "coming back down to earth." How can you find out if your life is "heading for the cliff" and you need to plot a new course? How can you get a "reality check?" Have the courage to ask a parent or close friend – they'll have the courage to tell you the awful truth because they care deeply for you.

LIFE LESSONS:

- There are important, fundamental life lessons.
- Learn these early, and your life will be improved immeasurably.
- Don't think you're special and the rules of life and laws of nature don't apply to you.
- Have respect for limits and boundaries.
- Live life in balance and in moderation.
- Your ego may lead you astray.
- Good decisions are not based on foolish pride and self-interest.
- Have you flown "too close to the Sun?"
- When (not if) you do, apologize and ask for forgiveness.
- Seek the strength and wisdom to make great decisions.
- Open your mind to the possibilities.
- Don't let success go to your head. Come back to earth.
- Act like you've been there, but don't act like you deserve it.
- Don't let your ego cloud your judgment.
- Let humility be your master. Listen twice as much as you talk.
- The saying goes – you'll find peace in your life when you're doing what God wants you to be doing.

2. BEST INVESTMENT

What if there was a secret investment that had the potential to change your life. What if this investment could provide returns that multiply over time? What if this secret was sure to pay big dividends? What if this idea didn't come from me, but from someone who actually knew what they were talking about? Would you be interested? Would you listen?

A few years ago, a famous investor met with a group of students. After opening remarks, there was time for "Q and A." Invariably, the discussion led to the topic of investing and one of the students asked a simple, but direct question – "Tell me, sir, what's the best investment you could make?" I can just imagine the student's little mind whirring – I'm going to get a "free" stock tip from the master! This is great – just wait till I tell my parents when I get home tonight! "Hey Mom and Dad, better plunk down the home equity on Amalgamated Widgets – it's a "can't miss" prospect!"

Out of the universe of investment possibilities, the investor's response may surprise you. Did he suggest technology, growth stocks or gold perhaps, as a hedge against inflation? Maybe he suggested the insurance industry, because of certain tax advantages that can increase after-tax returns, such as the special treatment afforded "inside build-up?" Or, did he tell the students to buy a farm because it's a limited, but renewable, resource? Nope, none of these.

When asked for the one best piece of investment advice, the investor told the student to "invest in yourself – that's the best investment." The foundation of this investment is, of course, a good education. Who was this investor handing out free investment advice? None other than Warren Buffett of Berkshire Hathaway fame regarded locally as arguably the finest investor in Eastern Nebraska. The name of this program – "Buffett and Gates Go Back to School." Who did Mr. Buffett bring with him to the program at the University of Nebraska – a person playfully described as "an associate" – Bill Gates. Can you imagine being a business student and listening to two of the most successful business leaders of our lifetime? Two men who've literally changed the world? Who then, in the course of presenting their thoughts, offer you their one "secret" – to invest in yourself?

This led to a creative advertising campaign for the university featuring a billboard with a picture of Warren Buffett and the question "What's a good education worth?" University of Nebraska President James B. Milliken said "Warren has always credited his education at the University of Nebraska for giving him a great start, and we certainly concur with his advice to students that a college education is the best investment you can make." What if you can't follow Mr. Buffett to the University of Nebraska? Will you be disadvantaged? A sobering thought, to be sure. I'm confident even President Milliken would be gracious enough to concede there are other schools offering a great education.

My Dad viewed an education with equal importance as Mr. Buffett, but from an opposite perspective. Mr. Buffett got an education and used it to create a lifetime of advantage. Dad never did get an education and he felt the compounding pain of regret and disadvantage. Dad grew up on a dusty farm in Kansas and almost starved as a child. Forced to work in order to eat and arriving at school hungry each day, he barely had an Eighth Grade education. Harvest time was in the fall and planting time in the spring. That doesn't leave a lot of time left to regularly attend school and learn your lessons. He'd lament that "you can't learn on an empty stomach."

Dad lived through the Great Depression and the hardship left an indelible mark. A college education was never an option for him. Survival was his prime motivator and just when he seemed to be making some headway in his journey, other obstacles jumped up on his roadway of life. After surmounting hunger, his next challenge was the draft and World War II. That, of course, could be the subject of another book. Skipping ahead with the story, Dad survived the war, but ended up as a thirty-year-old man with a wife and daughter and no education, no job, no skills and no money.

At age thirty, he was at a dead end. Each day, he walked the streets of Wichita, Kansas looking for work. This continued for months. Did he eventually find a paying job? Actually, the answer was "no." After asking a jeweler for a job many times, he walked into the jewelry store and offered to work for the owner for a month without pay. He told the owner, "I'll work for you for free. At the end of the month, if I'm not worth anything, then don't pay me." Through sheer determination and perseverance, he did what Mr. Buffett suggested – he invested in himself. He was a self-taught jeweler. He learned a trade on his own. Everything he knew about making jewelry he figured out the hard way. Skills learned only through trial and error. Oh my, life served "hard side up."

Like most parents, Dad wanted his kids to have a better life. That didn't mean he'd be around the house to play catch. The harshness of life left scars and his prime motivator was to survive, pay the bills and "provide for his family." He didn't have the time or life skills to do anything else. He worked morning till night six days a week. In retailing, if you're not there for the customer, you're not doing your job. Taking time off to drive the kids to school or to attend a school activity was unthinkable. It wasn't a choice because it wasn't an option. Fear of failure and the memories of being without were powerful motivators. "Driven" doesn't even begin to describe it.

Without discussion, it was assumed we'd go to college. Our ticket to a better life would be a college degree. My sister, twelve years older, was first up. Her only option was to go to the university in our hometown. It didn't matter what her major was or what kind of grades she made. The objective was to get a degree so she could be a "college graduate." The only question was when she could leave home. Dad told her "you can't leave this house until you graduate from college." Talk about motivating a student! Understanding the message "loud and clear," my sister finished college in only two and a half years. She graduated at age twenty. The first person in our family to go to college whizzed through in record time.

In our later years, I asked my sister why she went through so quickly. "Easy," she said. "I was desperate to get out of the house and the sooner the better!" By the way, there's a lesson here for any parents with "boomerang" adult kids still living at home. Learn from my sister – if you're trying to get them to leave, make home life miserable enough and the kids will be gone in a flash! College in two and one-half years – done and gone!

Without realizing it, I took Mr. Buffett's advice. For me, it wasn't by choice, but necessity. As a college senior, I tried to get a job. Unfortunately, there were few jobs available and the offers went to either the summer intern or the other applicant with a class rank above me. (As an aside, I've found there's an almost endless supply of those "other people" who would perpetually snap up that last job opening just ahead of me!). So, with nothing in hand and nothing to lose, I applied to my hometown law school, the University of Nebraska. If I could get accepted, there was a definite upside – three more summers off!

What was interesting about this experience, as I look back, was Dad's perspective on my joblessness. During my college years, he never asked about my choice of major or my grades. He figured that was my responsibility and I should be pursuing my passion. He never worried about me finding a job, figuring my efforts would eventually lead to something. He was positive, but noncommittal. Dad could safely be described as the opposite of today's "helicopter parent."

There was one time he actually got excited about my accomplishments. It wasn't the day I graduated from college. No, it was the day I got accepted to law school. In his mind, on the day I received my acceptance letter, "Freddy was going to be a lawyer." He had no idea what going to law school was all about and he never asked about my grades or class rank. He didn't take into account the enormous uncertainties and obstacles that were ahead. After all, you had to pass the classes, write the papers and graduate from law school and then study for, and pass, the Bar Exam in order to be admitted to practice law. No, none of those substantial hurdles mattered. The obstacles, and chances of failure, were invisible. To him, if I got accepted I was in the proverbial legal "clubhouse." At that moment, "Freddy was going to be a lawyer."

His simple, almost naïve, view seemed odd at the time. As you might suspect, like other graduate programs, there's a high attrition rate in the first year. There are myriad reasons why a person doesn't complete a graduate degree – health issues, cost and lack of commitment, to name a few. Also, graduate school is very competitive and the goal is to get good grades, get a good internship and then land that plum job with a large firm. It's preordained that your only goal is to reach for the brass ring. Anything less than total competitiveness does not compute. It's all about the best grades and the best law job possible. At least, that's what you're led to believe.

After rejecting Dad's simple view for years, I've recently reversed course and come to embrace it. He was right – the goal is to get an education – "something they can't take away from you." Make yourself better. You don't necessarily need to do well and you don't need to be a practicing lawyer. In fact, law is an area that applies broadly throughout business life. What if you decide to do something else? What if you graduate, pass the Bar and go into business? What if you follow your passion and become a High School teacher? What if you go to work for a bank or securities firm? What if you become a real estate agent? What if you become a highly educated and talented volunteer at a homeless shelter? Won't you be better at these "non-law" jobs because you went to law school? The possibilities are endless and the benefits of law school profound. After all, once finished, you know how to listen, sift through the facts, make sense of the story, find the issues and then apply the applicable law. You also know how to write and how to argue. OK, so maybe the ability to "argue better" is not so good, but the other skills are valuable and applicable throughout life!

Even if law school is not on your radar screen, the point is to better yourself by getting an education. This may mean going to a trade school and becoming certified in a particular field. I believe air conditioning and pool repair specialists will always be in demand in Phoenix! You could attend a great two-year community college. You could start at a community college and, after gaining confidence, transfer to a four-year university. Your history major may lead to a job as a writer or journalist. Your love of math or science could lead you to become a teacher. You could decide that your true passion is cooking and go to culinary school. This, in turn, may lead you to open your own restaurant. How exciting would that be?

Again, the possibilities are limited only by your imagination and courage to improve. However, the options will be available only if you further your education. Simply, the investment in your education will pay off, but exactly "how" and "when" may come as a surprise.

A word of caution on the "get all the education you can" message. A caveat – a warning label. There's one thing you should be very careful about when it comes to your education. Incurring debt. I'm confident that, over your lifetime, an education will pay off. What I can't predict is how or when the pay-off will occur. On the other hand, I can state with certainty that if you borrow to attend school, your loan payments will start immediately and will not change to match your income. Basically, speculative borrowing has some serious downsides. Carefully analyze your education alternatives (state schools are less expensive than out-of-state tuition) and prepare a post-graduation budget based on the job/profession income levels. Then "do the math," and determine if you can afford the school/degree you're pursuing. If you can't, then I strongly encourage you to "think twice" and re-evaluate. Large school loans will impose a heavy burden on your life after school and they are virtually non-dischargeable. You'll be paying, literally, for the rest of your life.

Let's assume you've reached your goal and have your degree. Is that the end? Do you stop there? No, to maximize your potential, you should become a life-long learner. Even if you have a specific career, such as a banker, engineer or CPA, you can strive to be better. A professor told me that you don't really learn a subject until you've either taught it or written about it. He explained that learning a subject for a test at semester's end is only the first step. You'll take additional steps up the ladder if you write an article or teach the subject. The teaching can be in the form of in-house training or at a seminar. He believed you truly learned a subject when you knew enough to explain the subject and then could answer questions. I know you've been there, and it takes a lot of study and preparation to teach even the most basic course for thirty minutes. I can count the hours spent preparing (and worrying about the mistakes I'm sure to make in front of the audience!).

Oh, and while you're at it, being a life-long learner will have other benefits. It will make your current job more enjoyable and you'll feel more confident. As you invest your time, your job skills will increase and you'll become a better employee. You'll be sought out by others simply because you had the guts to stand up in front of the crowd and lecture on the subject. You'll also meet more people in the same line of work. Building a network of "smarter than you" friends/colleagues/mentors is especially important. They may be the source of your next "can you help me" question, or even the source that leads to your next position or job. Professional life is dynamic and unpredictable – so it's best to be armed with a lot of resources!

LIFE LESSONS:

- What if you could discover the best investment?
- Imagine learning one secret that will change your life.
- Imagine you could ask Warren Buffett for his best investment advice. Would you listen?
- The best investment is to invest in yourself.
- You invest in yourself by getting an education.
- An education is something "they can't take away from you."
- Dollars spent on an education are returned over a lifetime of earning potential. It's a huge multiplier.
- Any college will do and any degree will matter.
- Can you imagine anything more important to do with your life between the ages of eighteen and twenty-five?
- One caution: Be careful about borrowing/school loans. You'll be re-paying for the rest of your life (without regard to your income).
- Develop the skills of a life-long learner. Be curious.
- You'll learn a subject only when you've taught or written about it.
- Use your education to build a "smarter than you" network of friends.
- Unhappy in your current job? Go back to school. Qualify for a new job.
- Cake decorating, anyone?

3. GOALS

If you were planning to drive from Boston to Los Angeles, what would you do? You'd develop a thoughtful plan – starting with an itemized budget of the costs and anticipating the need for cash versus credit card. Get your car inspected and serviced to make sure it was ready for the journey. Prepare a checklist and pack everything necessary. Anticipate there may be problems and have a plan in case of emergency (do you know how to change a tire?), including a safety and medical kit. Study a map and carefully plan your route. Estimate distances to drive each day, and have reservations at motels along the way. Research places of interest you'll want to stop and see (I've known some who plan summer driving trips with stops at different ball parks to catch a baseball game) to make the trip more enjoyable. Then, confident and prepared – the day of departure would arrive and you'd start off with your favorite song blasting on the radio. Wait, did I forget the camera?

Is life different from a long car trip? Doesn't the detailed preparation for a long trip seem like common sense? Aren't all the steps obvious? Then, why does it seem like we're living life out of control and without a plan. Why do we put more thought into driving the next five days, than we do living the next five years? Why do we seem to pay more attention to our car, than to our life? As Yogi Berra probably said, "It's hard to know where you're going when you don't know where you're going!"

Imagine you're building a house. First, you'd start dreaming about the exterior design. Does your perfect house have two stories or one? Modern, rustic or "Santa Barbara" influenced? To bring your dreams to fruition, you'd start noticing interesting houses as you drive, spotting ones that have characteristics you find pleasing. Then you'd start on your floor plan. How many bedrooms and on which side of the house? Would the floor plan meet your needs – would it facilitate the way you live and interact? Would it have a "chef's" kitchen or would the kitchen be "open" and more of a place for the kids to congregate?

After you designed the house, the architect would take over and complete the blueprints, insuring that the house design met the building code. The architect would also complete mechanical, electrical and roof plans. A structural engineer would examine the structure and double check code compliance and make sure the house was structurally sound. Load-bearing walls must be strong and roof trusses perfectly placed. Experts at the city would scrutinize the plans to make sure the structure was safe and in accordance with local code. A house can't be built unless the design can actually "deliver" a safe structure that meets minimal standards.

Imagine if your life, your future, could be designed and constructed like a house. You'd carefully and methodically consider what other people do with their lives and determine which life you'd like. You'd ask a lot of questions about what others do for work and what they like/dislike about their life. Then, you'd blend in their experiences with your own passions and perspectives. You'd consult with friends/family that know you and ask for their opinions. Do they think you'd be happy or successful with this particular "life design" in mind? As you narrowed your possibilities, you'd be reducing your ideas to writing – a blueprint, if you will, of your life. Thereafter, you'd be required to consult with an "expert" to have your life plan "stress-tested" to make sure it meets minimal standards. Only if your life plan can pass a "reality check," would it be approved. If not, "back to the drawing board!"

So, how do you create a blueprint for your life? Like planning for a house, or preparing for a long car trip, your life journey must start with the end in mind. At age 40, what kind of life do you want – what does it look like? Are you a respected business owner whose passion for life has been quenched with entrepreneurial adventures? Are you in a profession – doctor/lawyer/clergy – governed by a code of ethics? Are you in the police force or in the midst of a fabulous career in the military? Are you a teacher, inspiring the minds of countless children and experiencing the richness of learning each day? Are you an advertising executive thinking up the silliest TV commercials – and getting paid for it?

In order to end up somewhere, you must start with the end in mind. To do that, you must have goals. Without goals – without the map or the architectural drawings – your life journey will be confusing and frustrating. You'll wander around for years without focus or direction. Later, you'll likely discover you're stuck in the same spot – the same job with the same pay – that you vowed to get out of. Has this saying ever applied to you: "I don't know what I want, but I'm sure I won't be happy until I get it!" Oh, my!

Without goals, the chances of progressing towards that great life you've imagined are not good. Would a coach enter a game without a specific and well-conceived game plan that has been clearly communicated to the players? Never. Why is the game of life different?

Recently, I took golf lessons from a remarkable teacher. The first lesson began with fifty minutes of talking and only ten minutes of swinging. I was surprised (not that a "quick fix" was in order – my game is much worse than that!). We sat down and he asked me about my goals. Looking for "benchmarking" data, he asked where my game was today and what my goal or objective was in the future. I had to think for a moment, because my goal had to be worthy, but realistic and achievable. Once my goal was agreed to, he gave me a pen and paper so I could identify and commit to the steps necessary to reach my goals. Specifically, how hard was I willing to work? Was I prepared to do the little things necessary – the things I didn't want to do at a time I didn't want to do them? Was I ready to sacrifice to accomplish the many little steps that, when added up, would increase my skill level? Was I ready to stop dreaming and start doing? Hey - this wasn't about golf, I discovered, this was about life!

How can you create a great game plan for your life? Begin by setting goals. However, it's not as easy as identifying one big goal. Without the benefit of scientific study or empirical evidence, I believe you should have three sets of goals. There are "big ones" to be reached many years in the future. There are "intermediate ones" that will take up many of the intervening years. Then, there are the most important goals of all – the little ones. Why are the little ones so important? Because these goals are tangible "action items." These short-term goals literally change the direction of your life. They require discipline and accountability. Starting to-morrow morning, get up earlier and exercise. Eat balanced meals. Study one extra hour. Be more focused, more determined. Deliberately choose the more difficult path and work longer and harder than your peers. Decide to change your major or enroll in community college. Without any idea how you'll pay for it, be determined to sacrifice everything to get that degree. After enrolling, begin searching for a part-time job to support your new life of effort and reward. Can you feel the power and excitement of a goal-oriented life?

How do you identify and set goals? By first looking inward. Who are you? What's your passion? What topics get you excited, causing your speech to be elevated and more intense? What are the characteristics of the "authentic" you – the ones that make you unique? What do you want others to say about you – what do you want to be known for? Who do you admire and why? Simply, what makes you happy, content and fulfilled – what's fun?

Start a goal-setting journal with three categories: "must haves," "don't want" and "what's fun." Keep it handy and write down your thoughts when the creative mood strikes. Be mindful and candid about your strengths and weaknesses. You'll be amazed at what your list reveals about your authentic inner self. From this journal, commit your goals to writing. Revise over time as reality dictates.

Goal setting is not just for the individual. A happily married couple recently told me one of their secrets for "couple success" was they set couple goals. Each year, on New Years Day, they prepare a list of things they want to do in the next twelve months. Then, they discuss their individual lists and compromise and agree on their "couple goals" for the next year. Their goals are limited to three to five items and their goals must be attainable and realistic. Can you imagine the bond and passion they re-ignite at the start of each year? Can you imagine the joy they have working together as a couple towards common goals? Wouldn't you want to be them?

A farmer never plants without first preparing the soil for a specific crop with a "bushels per acre" goal. Begin taking the small steps of preparation for your life journey. Start small, tomorrow. Ignite the power of intention within you. Maximize your potential. Live a fabulous, authentic life.

LIFE LESSONS:

- Are you living your life aimlessly, without a plan?
- Have you put more thought into the next five days, than you have the next five years?
- Are you in pursuit of what's urgent, not what's important?
- A great life, like a cross-country car trip, requires advance planning.
- You don't know where you're going, if you don't know where you're going.
- Design your life like you'd design a house.
- Imagine what you want to be in twenty years, and then work backwards.
- Dare to aim high. Dream big.
- Be in pursuit of your passion and purpose.
- Create a "blueprint" based on careful thought and research.
- Have your plan "stress-tested" by others who know you.
- Set goals.
- Divide into three: long-range/"big" goals; medium goals; and little goals.
- To be effective and actionable, your goals must be clear and specific.
- Little goals are the most important. They change the direction of your life. Work relentlessly to achieve them.
- Start working in a new goal-oriented direction tomorrow.
- Goals will ignite your power of intention.

- Reassess your goals annually. Adjust your dreams to changing realities.
- Are your habits the ones that lead to success?
- Find the fun.
- Live a fabulous, authentic life.
- Fulfill your destiny!

4. PERSISTENCE

Having read the story of Icarus, you're living a life of humility and gratitude. You understand the greatest investment is the one you make in yourself and you either have, or will obtain, an education. You've made a list of the things you want, researched your future and determined the characteristics of an authentic, fun you. Based on careful thought, you have a list of short and long-term goals and are working diligently towards them. You're in pursuit of your passion and purpose, sure to fulfill your destiny.

So far, your life has tracked steadily upward in perfect sequence and your "ducks are in a row." For years, you've prepared for that one interview with the perfect employer. Surely you'll just show up and that one dream job will be yours. The highway of life unfolds perfectly, and in order, right before your eyes, right? Not exactly.

Maybe you'll be the exception. Maybe you'll be the one to easily climb the ladder of success. Maybe you'll land the perfect job after the first interview. Then you'll stay at that one job for the rest of your working life. Maybe your success will come first and fast. I hope you're the lucky one and, if you are, I'll be the first to celebrate your easy path to success.

However, experience tells me life doesn't work that way. It seems unlikely that you'll interview in March, accept the offer in April, graduate from college in May and start work in June – and work at the same job with the same company for forty-three years until retirement.

Great things in life come with difficulty and a lot of effort. The higher the goal, it seems, the more time and effort required.

Simply, they're not giving away what you want in life. What you desire is not free. The job, career, profession that you desire must be earned through hard work, sacrifice and diligence. Reaching any goal, any objective worth having, takes enormous effort.

The challenges of life will grind you down. The laws of nature will conspire with human nature to make it tough. Things will happen to you that don't seem fair and, midstream, the rules will change. The road to success is littered with those who've failed or quit. In order to have any hope of achieving your goals, there's something extra required. Persistence.

In college, I asked business owners I respected what they wish they knew more about. Their answer surprised me. They said they wished they knew about taxes and how the tax system worked. This was important because it affected how they made business decisions. What type of entity (corporation or partnership) should they use? Were they always required to sell assets first, or could they exchange or swap like kind assets without paying any tax. The list goes on. Tax efficiency mattered because cash is critically important to a small business. Armed with this information, I thought that if I knew about taxes and could help businesses conserve cash, I'd be valuable to business owners and I'd have a job.

As it turned out, that was the easy part. The hard part was actually getting one of those jobs. In my senior year of college, I interviewed with three accounting firms and they hired the one or two people above me in class rank. Other companies hired from their summer interns. No job, no option. So, I headed off to law school. I interviewed with over thirty law firms in multiple cities during my junior and senior years, but discovered the same obstacles. There were only a few tax positions and they were filled by summer interns or by tax lawyers who went to New York University for a graduate tax degree. My choice was to give up on my dream or sell everything and move from my Midwestern home in

Nebraska to New York City to attend NYU. Stand on the shore and watch my dreams sail away or take the biggest plunge into the largest ocean. Since my dream was smoldering, but not dead yet, I booked a one-way ticket to NYC (no need for a car) and took the plunge.

After an extremely difficult year in New York attending the NYU Graduate Tax Program and another two years clerking for a federal judge in Washington, D.C., I finally landed a job with a law firm as a tax lawyer. That August, I returned to Nebraska to attend my ten-year high school reunion. My classmates asked me what I did and what I had to show for my career. My answer was "I don't know" and "not much." It took me ten years to find a job that I hadn't even started yet. It was funny to try to explain that I'd accomplished so little after so much time and effort. In fact, when people ask me what I do I respond: "I'm someone who knows so much about so little that is of interest to so few!" Yeah, that about sums it up.

Why didn't I give up and quit? I was tempted many times, but I'm from the Midwest and I believe you should finish what you start. Persistence. My dreams kept driving me. I'd get turned down and knocked down, but I'd get up again, stronger. Persistence. Well, you get the idea.

Is my experience closer to the exception or the rule? A fair question, to be sure. If I'm the exception, it means that big dreams and large ambitions should come with relative ease. If I'm closer to the rule, then, if you've set the bar high and are reaching for the stars, you'd better be prepared for some setbacks and disappointments on the tough road ahead. You'd better prepare for the long slog, with persistence firmly imprinted in your mind. The joke I've heard is that "Generally, it takes you ten years to become an overnight success!" My wish for you is that overnight success will be yours!

LIFE LESSONS:

- Great things in life come with difficulty and effort.
- Success generally does not come fast and first.
- They're not giving away what you want in life.
- The laws of nature will conspire with human nature to make it tough.
- The road to success is littered with those who've quit or failed.
- Prepare to get turned down and knocked down, but get back up again.
- Use adversity to your best advantage.
- In the military, you'd learn this: Every minute, you must do something to advance your position.
- Pursue your dreams with passion and persistence.
- Sometimes, your persistence – your drive to outlast others – will be the only thing you have going for you.

5. DECISIONS, DECISIONS

Recently, I met a famous college football coach in a hotel elevator. I asked him, after his years of coaching, what one piece of advice he had to offer. His response was simple and stunning: "You are the sum total of your decisions." He continued: "You made all the decisions that produced the "you" you're looking at in the mirror." He said it so quickly and so convincingly. I'd never thought of life that way, but it made perfect sense. Simple, yet profound.

Each day of your life, you'll be faced with many decisions. I believe it can be summarized like this: a person has choices and then decisions, with consequences to follow. It's the consequences – both good and bad – that add up and contribute to who you are as a person. When you see a pile of hay, it's nothing more than a lot of little pieces of straw gathered together. So it is with life – your appearance, morals, character, etc. – are the accumulation of a lot of little pieces, little decisions, put together. When added up, they become the "you" you're looking at in the mirror.

What will affect or influence your decision-making? Ultimately, your decisions reflect your priorities and values. If fitness is a priority, for example, you'll eat healthy foods. You've thought it through and connected the "cause and effect" relationship between healthy foods and a healthy body. You've done the "cost/benefit" analysis. You know "you are what you eat," and live accordingly. At the other extreme, a person with addictive behaviors will act in accordance with their priorities (as long as they can). The addictive cravings must be satisfied and their life will be geared to their addictive cycle. Similarly, a person with narcissistic tendencies will view life as being "all about them," and will make their decisions accordingly. So it goes – the examples are as varied as life itself, with outcomes predictable nonetheless.

Not surprisingly, no two individuals will have the same value system at the same time. One person's priorities will not be the same as another's. This fact can make life confusing and difficult because we tend to view everyone as equal and capable of seeing the world the way we see it. Just as you're unlikely to run into someone with the same eyeglass prescription, you're also unlikely to encounter others with the same values and priorities. In fact, they see the world differently and are equally confused at how you can't see their point of view. Others see life through the prism of their own glasses. Their decisions will reflect their priorities. It's not about you. You're not in control or in charge. The mistake is to think otherwise.

To better understand life and relationships, it's important to appreciate our differences. This fact alone may be a news flash to some. Our differences are magnified when we're required to function and cooperate together – whether in a business transaction, as co-workers or as a couple. If a group of co-workers, with deeply conflicted values, are required to work closely together to produce a new product, what is the probability of success? If you and I are co-workers preparing a joint report to our working group, and I like red and you like blue, what color will the cover be? The possibilities for differences and conflict are endless.

So, a not-so-small challenge is to understand and improve your own value system (which will improve your decision-making and make you better), while learning how others in your life, at work and home, are different. Be a detective and uncover their differences. Sure, you can ignore this – but do so at your peril.

A great life requires that you make difficult decisions. It takes courage to stand up for your own best interest. The "right" path is so often the harder one. How do you know when there's a "big" decision to be made and how do you make it?

I'm mindful that most decisions fall into the "small/everyday" category. I let my values guide these decisions and try not to spend too much time worrying about them. On the other hand, big decisions require serious and careful thought. They require input from others and a listing of "pluses/minuses." To make sense of life, I decided that a "big" decision was one that was either obvious (career, new job, where to live) or one that would foreclose me from making other choices down the road. For example, if I wanted to go to graduate school, like law or business, I'd better get good grades in college. My GPA mattered, and I needed to consult with the admissions staff to figure out the minimum requirements. If I didn't work hard enough to meet the minimum during my college years, I was eliminating my future options. It's never a good plan to be eliminated before applying!

So, take time to think ahead in your life and plan back in time. If there are minimum requirements in the way (minimum credit score to qualify for a home mortgage), you'd better identify them and perform accordingly. Be a thoughtful decision-maker. As you improve, your value system will also improve. The better you get, there's an added benefit – the less time you'll spend looking back, and the more effort you'll devote to the positive tasks of the day. Live life looking through the windshield, not the rear-view mirror!

LIFE LESSONS:

- You'll have choices, then decisions, then consequences.
- Your decisions will reflect your priorities.
- Constantly improve your value system.
- A great life requires that you make difficult decisions.
- It'll take courage – the "right" path is often the most difficult and lonely.
- We each see life through the prism of our own glasses.
- Understand and embrace the differences of others.
- For small decisions, let your values be your guide.
- For big decisions, take extra time to evaluate and enlist the help and support of others.
- Make your decisions and move forward.
- Worry is not a helpful energy. Live life looking through the windshield, not the rear-view mirror.
- You are the sum total of your decisions.

6. BIGGEST DECISION

There's one decision that is the single most important decision you'll make in your life. It looms large and must be viewed in the context of it's potential to affect your living years. It'll have a profound impact on your life and the path it takes. This decision will affect you literally for the rest of your life. It could impact everything you do, from your personal lifestyle to your financial future. It's so important it's being mentioned in a separate chapter. The stakes are enormous.

The biggest, most significant decision in your life is deciding on the person to marry. Think about the impact this one decision can have on your life. In the near term, it will directly affect the quality of your life. Will your hopes, dreams and goals be realized with the support of this one person, or will they be crushed in a heap of negative energy? Will this person sacrifice to build you up and feed you positive energy, or as a jealous narcissist, be intent on tearing your down? Will your life turn out to be one of the great love stories, or another country and western song title? If you want children, the decision of who will be the mother/father of your children becomes even more profound – and will affect you directly for at least twenty-one years, and indirectly for a lifetime.

A friend had one message magnetically stuck to the family refrigerator. No other messages or distracting handiwork were permitted. Growing up, he only saw one sentence. This message wasn't often discussed, because it didn't have to be. He got the point loud and clear because it was the only message delivered with consistency. The little magnetic sign read: "Who you marry is the single most important decision in your life." I was stunned to learn this and had never heard of parents communicating one message so clearly. Were they right? Yes, indeed. Did they get their point across without hounding and harping at their kids? Without question.

While deciding whom to marry involves both head and heart, and falling love is such a wondrous thing beyond description, at some point reality will set in. After the glow wears off and the affect of the love drug subsides, you're left with a new teammate for life. This person is, literally, your new best friend forever. If you had to pick a new best friend, like the one you have from grade school, does he/she have the characteristics you admire and respect? Does this person share your moral compass? The list of questions could go on and there are many great books on this topic to consult. Please read them to learn more from the experts.

Literally, you get one chance to get it right. How carefully will you choose? Forgive me for comparing a marriage to a car, but bear with me. Let's assume that at age twenty-five you get to pick one car that must last the rest of your life. Yes, there's a new "one car per lifetime" rule. If this rule applied to you, how carefully would you select your car? Would you rush for the shiny two-seat convertible or, after thinking it through, figure that some day you want kids and you'd better have a car to tote them around. You also like pets and need room for the dog. You may also need this vehicle for work, so a four-door pick-up may be more suitable. With each different car, you'd consult with friends and family to get their views: "What do you think, Mom and Dad? Tell me the truth!" Ultimately, you may find the best environmentally friendly four-door sedan that gets great gas mileage and say "Yes, that'll do it. I can fulfill my life's dreams with this car."

Would you spend time agonizing over every detail of your choices in cars and, thinking through the consequences and "pluses and minuses," make a well-informed decision? I'm sure you would. And if you were this deliberative, I'm confident you'd have made a great choice with a high probability of lifetime happiness and satisfaction. Is that how most of us evaluate the qualities of a mate? The divorce statistics, and country and western music song titles, tell us "probably not."

The decision is yours. Make a great one. My wish for you is that you may find a true best friend who shares your joys and sorrows and is with you until the end. I want your life to be a great love story. I want you to tell anyone who'll listen: "It's the best decision I've made in my life."

LIFE LESSONS:

- There's one decision that's the most important.
- Who you marry is the single most important decision in your life.
- Literally, you get one chance to get it right.
- If you plan to have them, who will be the mother/father of your children?
- Will your life turn out to be one of the great love stories?
- The divorce statistics say the odds are not in your favor.
- Find your one, true best friend forever.
- Be able to say: "I'm so lucky - that's the best decision I've made in my life!"

7. ADAPTABILITY

When I started as a lawyer, letters and documents were dictated and secretaries typed them out on a typewriter. Memory typewriters were just being introduced. This process placed a premium on accuracy, because changes to the document were not easily made (sometimes "cutting and pasting" and photocopying the finished page). Legal research was done in the law library, and the more difficult issues required a trip to a "big" library at either the university or State Capitol. Faxes didn't exist and all phones had cords. At that moment in history, the law business had been done essentially the same way for over forty years. The tools of the trade – books, typewriters and phones – remained unchanged.

Of course, you know the rest of the story. After 1980, things changed rapidly and fundamentally. The advent of the personal computer and the Internet made research and document preparation a snap. A cell phone and PDA make you accessible 24/7. Time has compressed in ways unimaginable – and if you can't serve the client at all hours, there's a competitor willing to jump in and take your place.

While I've experienced dramatic change in my brief career, what's in store for the next generation? I heard a teacher say recently that, by the seventh grade, our children have been exposed to more information than their grandparents were exposed to in their lifetime. This teacher also said our children would see more technological advancements in the next thirty years than the prior two generations combined. I haven't done the research to confirm, but it doesn't sound too far-fetched. With data compressed and digitized, it's clear we're on the edge of a new explosion of information. And that's just one aspect of the boom in technology.

This means my ninth-grader is so far ahead of where I was at his age, there's no comparison. It seems his life is beginning at a point where mine left off – which means he's racing ahead – and skipping a generation. If there's one constant in his life – it'll be change.

With this as a given, what will be required? It will be a combination of understanding, vision and adaptability. Understanding and accepting that change is both rapid and inevitable. Having the vision to spend more time looking ahead than looking back. Then, as the future unfolds, having the ability to adapt quickly to the new environment.

There's one thing that won't change. It's human nature. A friend likes this saying, and he repeats it with a knowing chuckle: "Human nature is the one thing in life that never disappoints." This is why the story of Icarus, and other tales of ancient Greek Mythology, will always be relevant. No matter how much changes, human nature will remain the same. This is why, the joke goes, we're tuned to the same radio station: WIIFM (what's in it for me).

The next generation is presented with an added, and difficult challenge. You must live a life filled with change and strengthened with adaptability, while comprehending the depths of human nature. A daunting balancing act, but one you're now prepared for!

LIFE LESSONS:

- A seventh-grader has been exposed to more information than their grandparents were in their lifetime.
- There will be extraordinary change in the next thirty years.
- Are you prepared for a life where change is the rule, not the exception?
- Prepare to look back to learn from recent history, but understand that a particular way of thinking may be "out of date" and even "obsolete."
- Approach life with change as an expectation.
- Develop a vision for the future. Use your imagination.
- Be adaptable.
- Understand there's one thing that won't change: human nature.
- Human nature will never disappoint. Don't be fooled to think otherwise.
- Live a life strengthened with adaptability, but prepared for the challenges of human nature.
- This knowledge is power.

PART II:
BUILDING YOUR
BRAND

8. IT'S ABOUT PEOPLE, NOT MONEY

What is business about? Is it about the pursuit of profit? Is it about creating a superior product or service that others are willing to buy? Is it about carefully managing the bottom line so that your business continues, survives and prospers even during difficult economic times? Is it a world in which "fair" is irrelevant and cold, brutal efficiency is the ultimate force that determines winners and losers?

Well, it's all of these, to be sure – but if you only focus on the metrics, you're missing a critical piece of the puzzle. Indeed, I believe you'd be missing the most important aspect that should serve as your guiding light. Get this right, and I'm confident you and your business will be more successful and you'll enjoy a richness never imagined.

I believe a fundamental principle of a successful business can be summed up like this: It's about people, not money. I imagine a pyramid of business success and the first and foundational layer at the bottom is "people." This is true for many reasons and on multiple levels. I'll explain.

I've yet to meet a successful person who's accomplished their goals without the help of others. Granted, I haven't done the research, but I haven't heard of a person who's achieved success alone. In fact, the common links in the stories of success revolve around a teacher, mentor, parent, coach or friend who've helped them during the early years and encouraged them before there was any glimmer of success. I'm indebted to many teachers and friends who, to this day, continue to be there for me and encourage me to be better.

If we needed others to get where we are today, why would the equation change once you experience success? If others helped you, aren't you duty-bound to repay the debt? When it comes to people, do you act more like Icarus, or are you humble and thankful for the gifts you've been given? Do you remember those who had a part in your path to success and honor their legacy by helping others?

It's possible to be cold, heartless, and tough and make a lot of money at the expense of others, but I don't think that's a winning strategy. Eventually, you'll run out of others to "run over," and the equation turns. When it does, you're going to need others and "they" will either remember or find out about your reputation. Yes, it's a small world and we each have a reputation. What will yours be? What do you want others to say about you? A deep and interesting question – and one that more than a few have not stopped to ponder. This bit of common sense may not be all that common.

Dad was a jeweler. For fifty years, he hammered, bent and melted gold into beautiful jewelry. He learned quickly that customers were precious and easily lost to the competition. Dad's secret strategy: make everyone glad they did business with you. Leave each person with a lasting, positive thought about you. Do this one-person-at-a-time for fifty years, and you'll have an amazing reputation.

No matter whether you're an employee or owner, whether you're in sales or whether you're convinced you're so lofty that you're immune from the vicissitudes and vagaries of life, you'll have a reputation. This reputation is your currency with people. You can ignore the value of your "people currency," but that's not good business.

I have one final people thought to share. If you find yourself as an employer or supervisor, you'd better treat your people better than you treat your customers. Why? If your goal is to have well-served, professionally treated customers who want to do business with you more than once, you'd better have well-trained, professional employees doing the serving. Your employees are the face of the organization. If they are unhappy, it will show. Customers are very perceptive, and they will feel the undercurrents. Thus, you have little hope of happy customers unless you've invested a lot of time and effort to create and maintain happy employees. People first – your own.

LIFE LESSONS:

- Business success is more than money and profits.
- Discover the secret and enjoy a richness never imagined.
- It's about people, not money.
- A person cannot achieve success alone.
- There are, and will be, many others who contribute to your success.
- Honor their legacy by doing your part and helping others.
- Your reputation is your "people currency."
- What do you want others to say about you – what do you want to be known for?
- Make everyone glad they did business with you.
- Make a friend before you make a sale.
- Treat your employees better than you treat your customers.

9. MENTORS: EVERYTHING'S BEEN DONE BEFORE

There are some elements of your career that are critical to your success. One of those elements is having a mentor. It may be possible to have a successful career without a great mentor in your corner, but the odds are surely stacked against you. There are three aspects of mentorship you should be aware of. First, get one in your profession to help you learn and improve; Second, each time you try something new, a new business or profession, you should find "short-term" mentors to help you get started; and finally, you are duty-bound to actively seek out those younger and be a great mentor in return. Mentorship is reciprocal: it must be asked for, received and then passed on from generation to generation.

Historically, many professions, law included, were learned through an apprenticeship. If you were interested in learning a trade and possessed the necessary skills, you found an experienced practitioner and went to work as an apprentice. You worked for low wages for a period of years and, in return, were taught the "tools of the trade." Since you weren't paid much, your employer had the luxury of taking it slow and teaching you step-by-step. You'd literally watch as the experienced "master" performed. You'd also do the menial tasks necessary to keep the shop running which added to your value proposition. Value given and value received: each side benefitted from the arrangement. By the end of your term, there's no question you were prepared to carry on your trade in the "real world" – because you were gradually given "real world" experience. You knew you could do it – because you'd been doing it under the watchful eye of an experienced practitioner.

As the pace of business advanced, there was less time to train apprentices. Gradually, the practice has been phased out. However, the practice of law has a steep learning curve, and learning gleaned from those more experienced is imperative. In recent times, most training is done in a law firm environment. With fewer firms hiring fewer lawyers (as a percentage) over the years, and with associate salaries going up, there's increased pressure to make the associates more productive, more billable, as soon as they start. This means less time available to "teach" how to be a practicing lawyer. Unfortunately, the learning curve is getting longer, not shorter, for young lawyers today. I'm sure this is true for virtually all professions. The economic pressures are unrelenting, while the need to learn the practical skills are even more important.

Whether you find yourself in law, business, medicine, teaching or computer technology, to name a few, your first goal should be to find a mentor. When you begin your career you quickly realize how much you don't know. The learning curve looks steep and perilous. This places an additional premium, as if one was needed, on finding a great mentor.

Ideally, this person is in your chosen field and is respected by his/her peers. It might be a person with slightly more experience on your work team or it might be a supervisor or member of management. Since a mentorship requires human connection, be prepared to have some "mentor" setbacks. Establishing a mentor relationship is more art than science and requires you both to feel a shared bond. But great things in life are not obtained without effort and persistence, so get focused and make this a priority.

If you have doubts about the importance of a great mentor, do you realize that even extraordinarily successful people have mentors to rely on and call for advice? Reportedly, Microsoft co-founder Bill Gates has a mentor. As a possible indication that business life, at times, mirrors the playground of our youth, he was already wildly successful when he picked his mentor. As a billionaire at the time, he must've got the imaginary "first pick." His choice: Warren Buffett, Berkshire Hathaway. According to reports, Warren and Bill spend time together talking about life, business and bridge. Except, it may not be in that order. They'd probably rank playing bridge first.

You shouldn't be limited to one mentor. You can have others who play a critical role in your path towards success. It's important to realize that everything you'll do in your life has been done before. Virtually everything you'll try or accomplish has been tried and accomplished by others before you. This is hugely important – because, if you're starting out or trying something new, there's always someone in your field who's gone before. There are many who'll lend a hand if you ask for their advice. These mentors are worth their weight in gold, because they've either made or seen all the mistakes to be made. They can literally guide you through the minefield of business and keep you on the path to success. They can dramatically shorten your learning curve and possibly even save you from impending disaster. Find them and invite them to lunch! Quickly!

Bill Gates has Warren Buffett. Luke Skywalker had Yoda. In my imagery of a more perfect life, my "Yoda" would be a farm dad I could call up for advice and counsel. He'd be wise beyond his years and sought out by all for simple words reflecting an extraordinary depth of thought. But, be careful what you wish for. Yoda had harsh words for Young Luke Skywalker and I imagine my farm dad would give me words of "tough love." He'd tell me to spend less time worrying about what others thought and more time on the task at hand. His parting words would reflect a recurrent theme: "Keep your head down, boy."

Imagine the following situation. Assume I was raised on a family farm in Nebraska. Over the years, Dad had accumulated a lot of acreage (debt free, of course). I left and went off to the big city to attend college and then law school. My brother stayed to work on the farm. Dad wants to keep the farm in the family for generations to come and is concerned about estate taxes being so costly that my brother and I will be forced to sell the land. In the fall of 2009, we have the following conversation:

Lawyer Son: "Hey Dad, you know how you've been concerned about the increasing value of land and the problem of having enough money to pay your estate taxes at death?"

Farmer Dad: "Yeah, son. I've seen that happen to others and it's a shame."

Lawyer Son: "And it's still your wish to pass on the farm to me and my brother, right?"

Farmer Dad: "That's right. What's your point?"

Lawyer Son: "Well, you won't believe this, but the current estate tax is due to expire. That means there won't be any estate tax for those dying in 2010."

Farmer Dad: "You mean no taxes due for anyone dying in 2010?"

Lawyer Son: "That's right. So, I may be givin' ya a call and invitn' ya to go huntin' next year."

Farmer Dad: "Son, I think I may be taking you hunting first and doubling your brother's inheritance!"

LIFE LESSONS:

- Apprentices got real world experience by working in the real world.
- The learning curve in your profession is getting longer, not shorter.
- When you start, you quickly realize how much you don't know.
- First Objective: find a great mentor.
- Your mentor should be a respected, experienced professional in your line of work.
- Mentorships require a personal connection. This will require persistence on your part.
- Don't be limited to one. Find others along the way.
- If you're considering a new line of business, finding a new mentor with experience/expertise can be critical to your success.
- "Everything's been done before," so find others more experienced and rely on their "been there/done that" wisdom.
- Be prepared: a great mentor may also provide a coach's "tough love."
- A good mentor/coach will tell you what you don't want to hear at the precise time you don't want to hear it.
- Welcome the criticism and turn it into a positive.

10. LEARN TO

There are many little things you need to learn. These things are relatively simple and easy to explain. Many are common sense; some reflect wisdom and others border on "tough love." However, I've never seen them discussed in a direct, "less is the new more" format. They are important and should be listed, so that you can go back and check every so often. I need a periodic reminder of my "lessons," and I'm sure you're the same way. Like Icarus, I need a dose of humility so I can be "brought down to earth." I learned most of these the hard way and want to offer them to you, so you can learn the "easier" way!

Here's an inexact, and I'm sure incomplete, list of things you need to "learn to." If you can "learn to" do (or not do) these things, your life will be a lot smoother and, hopefully, make more sense. Learn these sooner, and you should have a head start on the competition.

A fabulous life awaits you, so let's head off to training camp. The goal is to accelerate your "life" learning curve. Let's get started.

Fail. Wait a minute, you say! This is about positive lessons that are meant to help. Starting with failure is not helpful! True, but I want to get your attention and focus on the role failure will play in your life. Understand this, and it will help you to survive and prosper (my goal here).

Failure will play a role in your life in at least three different ways: (1) In order to grow and reach your potential, you must get out of your comfort zone and risk failure. If you have high self-confidence and self-esteem, you'll understand that taking calculated risks are a necessary part of a life well lived. You'll know that you won't succeed at everything you do and you'll be prepared to get knocked down, and get back up stronger; (2) you learn far more from your failures than you learn from your successes. Failures often occur for a reason, as a necessary part of your growth path, eventually building the skills you need to succeed. Failures teach you valuable life lessons; and (3) the minute you start a new relationship, job or career, you're on your way to a break-up, losing your job/career or getting fired. Thus, you must begin any new stage of your life, be it personal or professional, with the expectation that it will end poorly, abruptly or both. Understanding (and not denying) this will empower you to be proactive and begin to plan for the next, inevitable, life event – one that is higher/better. This knowledge may be the catalyst for building a great network of friends in your industry who may be the source of your next job/opportunity/reference. You may resolve to engage in continual "resume building" activities. Ultimately, your internal unrest may cause you to obey your "gut feeling" and say, "I'm an entrepreneur at heart." As a result, in order to fulfill your destiny, you may change your life's direction and set about creating your own venture/business/company.

Make failure your friend. Use adversity to your advantage.

Listen. In my line of work, listening is a critical skill. In order for me to do my job as an advisor, I need to listen to my client. I need to learn about the facts and her hopes/goals/objectives. Without understanding, I might provide advice or encourage a course of action that could prove to be misguided or wrong. To this day, I need to remind myself to listen to not only hear the story, but to understand. I must ask a lot of questions before I can decide on a proper course of action. Invariably, when I'm ready to jump to conclusions, I've missed the mark in some way. When I'm quick to assume, I most often get it wrong.

Listening is important in every line of work and it affects every personal and professional encounter. Have you been in this situation: "If only I'd listened, I wouldn't be in this mess." I have, many times. In fact, to counteract my tendency to talk before thinking, I repeat these words: "God gave me two ears and one mouth, so I can listen twice as much as I talk." Follow this advice – listen first, and listen twice as much as you talk. It will save you enormous time/money/frustration. Simply, talking too much, and first, will likely inhibit your success in your personal and professional life. If you don't believe me, ignore this advice and let me know how it turns out for you. I'd love to hear your stories!

Think Before You Speak. It's important to pause before speaking and ask yourself: what do I want to convey? Am I trying to frame a question, and, if so, what's my goal? Am I trying to learn something or impart information to others?

Thinking before you speak has other benefits. It should save you from saying things that don't make sense, or worse. After pausing, I try to speak clearly and in measured tones. I realize that how I say something is often as important as what I say.

Mark Twain said it best: "It is better to keep your mouth closed and let people think you a fool than to open it and remove all doubt."

Accept Criticism. After working at it for over twenty years, I'm a fairly good writer. But I didn't start that way. My first memos and documents I prepared were awful. My sentences were too complex and messages too long and convoluted (the joke is that lawyers get paid by the pound!).

I learned to write and then re-write because a law professor "bled red ink" over my papers. He'd criticize and critique until I couldn't take it. Then, he'd order me to edit my work and turn in a new draft in the morning. At the time, it hurt and I was frustrated. Later, I came to realize he did this because he cared enough to criticize and correct me. He cared about me and wanted me to get better – he wanted me to succeed. He invested in me, took the extra time and showed me "the error of my ways."

I owe my career to that law professor. He literally molded me into the writer I am today. In later years, we'd laugh about the "beatings" he administered and then he'd direct me to "pass it along," and mentor someone else. Throughout my career, he's held me accountable.

Get tough and do it quickly. Seek out others who'll give you constructive criticism. Have the courage to ask others what you need to work on to be more successful. Criticism, done constructively, is an important gift. It can accelerate your learning curve and propel you farther than you can imagine. You'll be richly rewarded if you find a great friend/mentor to help you. Chances are, they're already in your life just waiting for you to ask for their advice. Seek them out.

Ever notice the bothersome traits/habits/characteristics of others that stand in their way? Turn the tables. You have yours too – uncover them and correct them quickly as you speed ahead on your exciting life journey. The only thing holding you back is yourself not letting you go forward.

Put your ego aside and find ways to constantly improve.

Not Take It Personal. I started my career striving for excellence and caring about what other people thought of me. Worse, I wanted to be liked. When things went wrong, I thought it was my fault. I thought I was in charge and in control. Perfection seemed to be attainable, albeit just out of reach. This combination took its toll on me and caused my emotions to rise up and down like a roller coaster. I was under constant stress and my over reaction didn't help. I took it personal.

The fact is, it's a big universe out there and you are a very small part of it. The truth is, life is not personal. It just is. Things happen and go wrong for no reason – that's life. So, don't take it personal. Convince yourself that "it's not about you." If you do make a mistake (and we all do, since we're human), own up to it and apologize. Then, move on. Taking additional time and energy to "take it personal" is not going to help the situation. It's a negative, draining exercise.

While I haven't done the research, I believe there are three types of people in the business world. Those who care deeply for you and are genuinely interested in your success (a precious few), those who have no investment in you and really don't care (the vast majority), and those who believe you are in their way and need to be run over so they can get what they want at the moment (the size of this group "out to get you," can very depending on your perceived power, position or authority). If these two large groups of people don't care about you and have nothing invested, why should you care? If they don't care about your feelings, why do you give them any power or influence over yours? If you could ask them "is my interaction with you personal," they would say "no." So, if it's not personal to them, why is it personal to you?

Care deeply about what the first group thinks about you. To this small, and easily identified group, you should be highly accountable, apologize for your transgressions (when they occur), and use their collective strength and wisdom to build yourself up. For the rest, the fact is they don't care and it's not personal. You're not that important and don't fool yourself into believing otherwise. You have the keys to your emotions and don't give them your permission – your keys – to negatively impact you. Put up a deflector shield so strangers can't get in. Keep your emotions in balance and focused forward.

I wish it weren't so, but bad things happen to good people. Be prepared and resolve to be resilient. It's not personal. Do yourself a big favor – don't make it so.

Stop Digging. Do you know the first thing you're supposed to do when you find yourself in a hole? The answer is: stop digging. While this may be an old joke, the message rings true. The first thing you should do when you find yourself in a difficult situation is to stop the actions that are contributing to, or causing, the problem. Simply, if you're in a hole, you're there because you dug it yourself. Before you can think your way out of a problem, you need to stop your old way of thinking – the exact thinking that got you into this mess in the first place. You can't start thinking in a new way, or in a new direction, until you stop your old pattern of thought. Recognizing this, and then starting off in a new direction will be a profound "ah ha" moment in your life.

When you look around and discover you're in a deep hole – you know what to do. Throw the shovel down!

Be Patient. This is very difficult for me. While I can be slow to make up my mind, once I've reached a decision, I want it "as close to yesterday as you can get." I want what I want and I want it now. My urge for immediate action is enforced and encouraged by current society. Most of the new products are intended to "save time," or help us to do more with less. A TV show runs through an entire plot in sixty minutes and movies are completed in less than two hours. The commercials promise that we'll instantly look better/younger/slimmer or your money back. Everything we see and hear is geared towards instant gratification. When's the last time you spent two hours of uninterrupted time reading a book?

While I want what I want when I want it, the reality is that life is a cycle and I'm an infinitely small little cog. Whether it's the four seasons, the phases of the moon or the ticking of our biological clock, the cycles of life are unbending and universal. If you have doubts, read Chinese or Greek philosophy written thousands of years ago – it's as relevant today as it was then. For example, it was probably Confucius who said: "In the battle between the water and the rock, the water wins – because of its persistence." You can't bend the will of nature to meet your needs, and if you try you'll end up frustrated and exhausted – or worse. Are you the water or the rock?

Each case or project you work on will have it's own cycle. An organized business will prepare a "timeline" with a critical path of events. Each must be accomplished before the next "milestone" can be reached. An experienced manager will carefully develop these plans because the company's budgets and goals literally depend on them. Success will be measured each week to determine whether the focused execution is keeping the project "on time" and "under budget."

Even the smallest thing you work on, the most minor negotiation, will have it's own time frame and it's own cycle. The better you understand the problems and limitations of the other side, the greater your chance of success. Things take time and you shouldn't unduly rush them. To do otherwise, will put your request or objective at risk. People and organizations have a certain tempo for operating and you must allow them to complete their process. Sometimes it will allow them to "build consensus" and other times to "change direction." Either way, you must get out of the way. Your patience and understanding will invariably be rewarded. Slow and steady wins the race.

Yes, patience is indeed a virtue. Be patient. It's something I remind myself daily.

Do Things Right, Not Fast. Building on your resolve to be patient, you must also learn to do things "right." Life is filled with pressures and deadlines and there are temptations and motivations to get it done and out the door. It's "good enough" and besides, no one will ever notice the little details. However, without the details, the little things, your work will be mediocre at best.

If you are the product of your decisions, then your work is the product of little details. Leave them out and you'll be average.

Excellence will elude you. What do you want your reputation to be – what do you want to be known for? If you want your work to stand out and your customers to be happy they did business with you, then there's no choice. The pursuit of excellence requires you to think about each project, each thing you do, as an orderly progression of details. Skipping some of the steps, some of the details, is unthinkable. The details make the difference.

I worked on a road construction crew in college. Most of our work ended up being covered by concrete or graded over with dirt. So, it would've been easy to take shortcuts. For example, we could've saved time by installing steel rebar that wasn't straight and in perfect alignment. However, that was unthinkable for our boss, the construction crew foreman. He'd say: "Boys, we have pride in what we do, so make it pretty!" The notion of steel bars being "pretty" sounded funny, but we understood. Oh, and for the few workers that didn't get the message – they were fired.

Doing things right takes time, effort and discipline. It's not easy. Sometimes, the additional processes or steps involved will cause delays (or worse). When you first discover these delays, communicate with your team and with your superior. Don't place the burden on yourself. This knowledge is important and should be shared. Let the boss know about the facts and let the boss figure out how to proceed. Sometimes an early call to the client or customer to let them know that the promised delivery date will not be met is an important part of "client service." Then, offer to work extra hard to be part of the solution, not part of the problem. Additional creativity may be required and "above and beyond" steps necessary. I've often hand-delivered documents to my client – personally dropping them off at their office or home after hours.

Dad made rings by hand, literally hammering and carving the gold into a unique design. This was a slow and tedious process requiring great skill. Most rings today are made with melted gold poured into wax castings. He didn't like that method, because hammered gold has the most shine and lasts longer. He had a display case full of mass-manufactured rings, but didn't sell many. He couldn't stand to sell them, because their quality was inferior to his hand-made rings. This created problems because he was passionate about customer service. If, for example, a customer would drop in on Friday and say he needed a ring by Saturday afternoon (and he lived thirty miles away), Dad would say "No problem!" He'd drop everything and start on the ring in the afternoon and work into the evening. Then, excited, he'd wake up at five a.m. and be at work by six. Finishing by early afternoon, he'd then hop into his car and drive thirty miles to personally deliver his creation. The customer was stunned and so appreciative. Over the years, I heard this same story repeated a hundred times.

Dad's lessons about customer service and the drive to create lasting quality should be remembered. As our world gets smaller and more competitive, it will be the little things that differentiate and keep your customers or clients coming back for more. Take his lessons and apply them to your life's work. If you do things right, and not fast, you're destined to have a great career. Your reputation for excellence will, over the long haul, be rewarded.

Stay Cool Under Pressure. With experience as my guide, I can assure you that certain things will happen in your life. I may not be able to predict the timing or order, but I can guarantee you'll not be spared certain life events. One of them is that things will not go your way. The tide will turn and you'll be surrounded by adversity. Things go wrong, sometimes terribly so. I wish it weren't true and I hope you'll experience less than your share. Things large and small will go sideways, sometimes at the worst of times, in your personal and professional life. The question is not whether things will go wrong, but how you'll respond.

With years of difficult circumstances and things going wrong in my life in ways I never could've imagined, I've learned the hard way. I was unprepared for the tough times, which then caused the adversity to be worse and last longer than necessary. My goal is to make my emotional road a little smoother, with smaller potholes and dips that aren't as deep or long lasting. To do this, I had to accept that things go wrong because they're supposed to. Adversity is part of life and the sooner you can embrace this, the easier it will be for you to handle it more effectively. If someone at work tells me that "Things are bad, mistakes have been made and it's serious," I can only respond: "Of course!"

When things go bad, your first reaction should be to remain calm under fire. When the temperature goes up, your blood pressure should go down. When it gets hotter, you should get cooler. Why? There are many reasons. First, you must think your way out of trouble, and if you're running around with your hair on fire, you will not be thinking clearly. If you panic, your blood pressure goes up and breathing restricts – and you'll be less capable of processing and evaluating information as it comes whizzing by. Decision-making is at a premium and you'll need to do your best thinking in times of stress.

Second, everyone around you will be watching how you react. If you yell/scream/blame, you've virtually assured a bad situation just got worse. Your team will either run for cover or follow your lead and yell/scream/blame others. Neither will help the team react under stressful conditions and be conducive to creative problem solving. Finally, leaders must display calm resolve in times of crisis. If not, your leadership position will evaporate. A leader must always be focused on the way forward, not on how bad things may be at the moment.

Life is dynamic and unpredictable – and an important life skill is how you'll react and adjust to the changing circumstances. Seldom does anything go according to plan – so expect to be frequently tested.

Learn to stay calm under pressure. Prepare and practice your response. You can't control what happens, but you can control how you respond. It is the moment of your response to adversity that reveals your character. When things get worse, do you get better? What will the tough times and difficult experiences reveal about you (and what will you learn from them)?

Say "No." Learning to say "no" may seem like an odd skill to acquire. However, you'll no doubt be a "doer" who's motivated to improve your own life and the world around you. You'll have a positive "can do" attitude and a "no mountain is too high" mentality that will serve you well most of the time. You'll have the drive and intelligence to do many tasks at once. Thus, your strengths and positive character will cause others to seek you out – and indelibly move you to say "yes" to anyone who has a good idea at the time.

Your "Job 1" is to engage in self-care and self-development. Your job is to raise the best "you" possible – a person who reaches his/her full potential with the unique skills and abilities God has given you. To accomplish this, you must stay focused and make decisions (and sacrifices) that align and support your life goals. A tall task, to be sure, but one that will require you to do something that's contrarian: Say "no." You have limited time/money/energy and you must turn down many opportunities and even worthy causes. Your daily decisions will ultimately determine what happens to you – whether you succeed or fail. So, resolve to make daily decisions that are aligned with your success. This may require you to say no to friends and colleagues, but a great life requires difficult decisions. You may disappoint those you love or respect, but it will be a necessary part of your advance towards adulthood and, ultimately, success as you've envisioned it.

Practice and prepare to say "no." Prepare to disappoint others along the way and not join in their worthy causes. You have your own great life in progress and you need to stay "on task." Paradoxically, the greater your talent/ability/compassion, the more you'll be sought out by others yet the less time you'll have to devote to them and the harder it will be to say "no." Understanding this paradox will be of great value.

Let Go. This may be a shock, but you're not in charge and not in control. There are higher forces at work in the universe and nature will take its course. God has a plan and, in order to live a healthy and productive life you must do two things: (1) engage in self-care so you can reach your full potential and fulfill your destiny; and (2) get out of the way, so as not to interfere in God's work.

There may be times in your life when you are violating one or both of these rules. You'll know because you'll be tired, weary and exhausted from the daily struggles. Everything's an effort and even simple tasks are difficult. There are things you desperately want in your life – like reaching that ultimate career goal or raising that "perfect" child – and you'll never be satisfied until you grab the proverbial "brass ring" of perfection. Your burdens will be made even heavier by the additional baggage you carry with you – like jealousy, fear, anger or the desire to get even for the wrongs done to you by others.

I can't explain why, but experience tells me that you must "let go" before you can "have." You must overcome your fears and anxieties and surrender your misguided perception that you're in control. You must "let go" before you can truly love others and before you'll ever achieve success. Life is not a linear path upward in a straight line, and all your efforts to change the inexorable forces of nature will not be successful.

Learn to "let go." When you do, your spirit will be freed to ride the river of life – and you'll experience the joy in the journey. The saying goes – you'll find peace in your life when you're doing what God wants you to be doing. When you're acting consistent with God's plan, the challenges will not seem so great, and the daily tasks not so difficult. The alternative: stand in the river and perpetually walk up stream against the current. Oh, my!

Live in Balance. Hardly a week goes by, it seems, when another scandal's revealed. The stories all sound the same. A businessman or investor started honestly but then something happened that caused this person to take unnecessary risks. This, in turn, caused the "lying, cheating and stealing" to escalate. The scheme always starts small and then spirals out of control. He/she just needed a little extra money, so the story begins, and had every intention of paying it back. It may be greed, ignorance, or both, but it seems there's a common thread underlying it all: a lifestyle that needed to be attained or maintained. Have you read about a financial scandal where the perpetrator lived modestly and below his/her means – or is the common thread to white-collar criminality about the exciting/lavish lifestyle that eventually precipitated their downfall?

Have you heard of these scandals occurring in farm country? I'm sure there may be one somewhere (humans being human, after all), but I don't recall reading about any farmers creating a Ponzi scheme to support the high life. The reason – they live within their means, don't like debt and are skeptical of the "too good to be true" claims of others. In short, they live off their land, pay cash, and don't buy what they don't need.

If the current financial crisis, and the Ponzi schemers who've been exposed by the downturn, teaches us anything, it should be this: live in balance. Don't strive for "too much, too fast," the largest house, fastest car (admittedly, this is hard for me, since I really like fast cars), or the most stuff (invariably purchased on credit). Live your life in moderation. Save your money. Be skeptical of the claims of others. Avoid the risks of the extremes. At a minimum, your temptation or motivation to do stupid things will be reduced!

Dad (who lived through the Great Depression) told me there are two ways to be rich: earn more or want less. Aren't farmers, who live a life wanting less, great examples of being rich? Shouldn't we be more like them?

Obey Your Body. You are given a remarkable vessel in which you'll live your life's journey. Your body is perfectly created in God's image. Like Icarus, you have the easy part. All you need to do is take care of it and obey a few simple rules. Nothing too difficult or strenuous, mind you. No task too tall – even the simplest among us can succeed with ease. It doesn't even take a degree in biology or biomechanics to figure it out.

Learn to take care of your body. Eat right, consume less junk food and eat more veggies. Substitute water for soda and avoid starch and processed sugar. Get eight hours of sleep on a regular schedule. Sleep is critical to your good health – it's the time the body repairs and rejuvenates. Get regular physical exams and keep your LDL low and your HDL high. Exercise and avoid the temptation of bad habits – such as smoking or drinking to excess. Heed the advice Daedalus gave to Icarus: avoid the extremes.

Learn to listen to your body. It will tell you when things are out of balance and overstressed. If some part of your body hurts or bothers you, obey the message and see a doctor. If your teeth hurt or your jaw aches, see a dentist and get your teeth fixed and bite properly aligned. Don't wait too long because any single problem can, over time, compound. Your body's speaking if only you'd listen. Nothing new here – sounds like common sense.

Express Your Feelings. If life came with an instruction manual, it would include a chapter on how to communicate and express your feelings. This chapter would help you identify your feelings and provide the skills necessary to communicate them with ease. But, life doesn't come with a manual and I've struggled with this life skill. My childhood interactions were not conducive to the expression of feelings. You didn't talk about them.

My wish is that you'll have fewer challenges, but then approach them with greater life skills. I want to shorten your learning curve with a "less is the new more" approach. With simplicity as our guide, I'd like to set forth a simple, direct strategy for communicating your feelings. If you've already mastered this skill – Hooray – you can skip this part of the book!

Here are the steps for successfully communicating your feelings:

Step 1: Ask for Permission and Be Open to a Time in the Future:

"I'd like to share some feelings with you and, if this is not a good time, then I'd like to schedule a time for us to sit down and chat."

Step 2: When You Start, Begin by Thanking The Listener for Their Time: "Thanks for sitting down and listening to me. I really appreciate it."

Step 3: Express Your Feelings:

"I feel [name the feeling … sad, confused, uncertain, upset]

About [describe what was done to you/or the situation]

Because [explain why it bothers you]."

Step 4: "Thank you for listening."

You must be able to logically describe a situation or event and explain why it bothers you. Your feelings are legitimate and should, in an appropriate and professional context, be expressed. Of course, don't make it personal and whining, naming or blaming is not allowed. The objective is to express legitimate feelings and be listened to and understood.

There is one final step to consider. What do you want? What are you asking for? Think carefully about the "end game" and spend extra time trying to figure out what a positive outcome looks like.

Apologize. As sure as the sun will rise tomorrow, you'll make mistakes in your personal and professional life. You're human and we all do it. The question is not whether you'll make mistakes, but when and how many. Most will be small, but every once in a while there'll be a whopper of a mistake that will require you to be fully accountable and responsible. You can't, and shouldn't, let these mistakes go by without facing up to them and doing the emotionally mature thing: apologizing.

Apologies should be brief and to the point. No need to belabor the obvious. Your words should convey that you are taking responsibility for your actions and empathizing with their position ("I understand you may be upset"), while not trying to make an excuse.

A simple personal apology goes like this: "I know [insert stupid thing here] bothered you, and I'm sorry I did it. I apologize. Will you forgive me? What could I do to make it better?"

A simple business apology goes like this: "You may not be aware, but I [did this stupid thing] and I'd like to apologize. I can't really explain how or why this happened, but I'm sorry it did." If it's to a customer, you may want to add: "I will make every effort to make sure this doesn't happen again," or "What can I do to make this situation right with you?"

Why do I mention apologizing as a "life lesson" to be learned? Because I've messed up too many times to count. I've had to learn this the hard way. It took me too long to figure it out, and I wish I learned it earlier!

Write Notes. Virtually everyone is overwhelmed with the volume and pace of information today. If you have a personal email account, you're getting messages from friends, information from schools and solicitations for discount insurance or roof repair. If you have email at work, the sheer magnitude of messages (plus attachments) is beyond your ability to read, assimilate and respond. In your lifetime, it'll only get worse.

There's one way to stand out from the crowd. Something old fashioned that's sure to get you remembered. Send a hand-written note on personal note cards. The written word is powerful, especially when expressed in ink. My goal is to send one hand-written note a week. Sometimes it's to thank a busy executive for meeting for lunch, other times it's to RSVP regrets for an invitation received. My notes have great impact. Often, the recipient will search me out in a gathering to say how much he/she appreciated receiving my note and how rare and special it was.

Buy your note cards and start your own "card a week" program. If nothing else, send a note to a dear friend expressing thanks for their friendship and being there to support you in your times of need. You'll instantly stand out from the crowd and be remembered. Isn't that part of your plan?

Tell the Truth. Wait, you protest – you learned this as a child. Your parents taught you that you must always tell the truth. Well, I'm from the Midwest, and my parents taught me the same thing. I had to tell the truth and this was especially true if the person asking was an adult or person in a position of authority. Later in life, that became problematic and a source of confusion as I launched into the working world. How do you transfer childhood teachings into the "rough and tumble" of the real world where there are others who don't share your moral bearings, don't have your best interest at heart and may be seeking information only to use it against you?

I naively started out believing that if someone asked me a question, I had to tell the complete and total truth about the situation. I didn't understand that a person must learn about nuanced speech – choosing words carefully, exercising discretion and, at times, simply refusing to answer. I was confusing not saying things that were false (which I won't do) with blurting out every single piece of truth as if I were on "truth serum" (which I shouldn't do). I needed to develop a filter of judgment and discretion, supported by the knowledge that there are times when refusing to answer is not only within the boundaries of "telling the truth," but the right thing to do.

"Telling the truth" is more about not uttering false words and less about how many words you speak. If you're going to say something, you shouldn't speak falsely. However, that doesn't mean you must answer or respond in the first place. As an adult with human dignity and self-respect, you're entitled to say less and can choose to refuse to speak at all.

I wish I learned this sooner: just because someone asks you a question, doesn't mean they're entitled to an answer. In addition, there are many situations where eventually you may discuss the subject, but not according to their time schedule. You can choose to answer a difficult question under difficult circumstances with the following: "I'm not prepared to discuss that topic at the moment;" or "I'm sure you'll understand that I'm simply not at liberty to discuss that at this time;" or "You'll need to get my bosses/clients/third parties permission first before I can comment." Then, that part of the conversation is over and you refuse to discuss any further. Even if the questioner hounds you for an answer, you can simply refuse and repeat your words. Of course, there are certain situations where you'll want to propose a later time to talk when you're better prepared to discuss the subject. But that's up to you.

Keep Your Word. If you tell me you'll meet me for lunch at 11:45 a.m., what time do you show up? If you commit to getting the project finished by 10 a.m. on Thursday, when do you complete the project? If you say "I'll call you tomorrow," when do you call? These are small examples, but they relate to the same question. Do you keep your word? Can you be counted on? Are you reliable and can you be trusted to follow-through without being reminded? Is your word/promise/commitment "as good as gold?" It better be, because your reputation depends on it.

If the lunch appointment is for 11:45, you'd better plan to arrive at the restaurant at 11:35. This allows ten minutes for minor delays. Make it a habit of being a few minutes early – it's a matter of respect and it's something to be known for. The alternative is that you may be starting out an important business meeting apologizing for being late. Not a great way to make a first impression.

Smile. I want people to like me, help me and remember me. In varying degrees, I need the assistance of others to accomplish my goals and objectives in life. I can't do it alone. At a minimum, the help of others will make my job a little easier – or possibly make the difference between winning or losing. I like feeling connected and believe that some part of my success is due to the help I've received from others.

I've developed a secret strategy. I smile. I smile at the store clerk, the office receptionist, and the manager of the sandwich deli where I eat lunch. I smile when I meet important clients to close a deal. It doesn't matter who it is – I smile at them all. Do you know what I receive in return? A smile. Yes, based on my informal research, I've concluded that smiles are contagious. Even if someone is not in the best mood, I believe I can get him/her to crack a smile, if only for a moment. Granted, there are some I meet who may require two or three of my smiles to get one of theirs – but I'm undeterred and determined to get a smile in return. I also believe I feel better when I smile and therefore assume they feel better as well. A win-win proposition if ever there was one.

Take my smile challenge and smile at everyone you meet for the next week. I predict you'll feel better and get many smiles in return. Also, a smiling person is more inclined to help/assist you – and isn't that what you need to succeed in business and life in general?

If you have doubts, consider this example: you're in a restaurant and the server greets you with a smile and is happy to wait on you. The next time you return, she remembers your name and what you ordered. The third time, it's her day off and your new server is grumpy and doesn't smile. Who will get the bigger tip? I'm confident the amount you tip depends on the quality of the service. Make no mistake, if you're in the service business earning tips, the amount of tips you receive will be directly related to your smile. If that's true for servers, why isn't it true for other business relationships?

Love Yourself. Of all the things I've suggested you need to learn, this one may prove the most elusive. It seems the hardest task is to focus inward and give yourself the kind of love you so freely give to others. Not just once in a while or when you're reminded, but on a constant basis. Yes, self-love is something missing yet something so desperately needed. You especially need it during the tough times, when you feel unloved and unworthy of love. Like water in the desert, it's required to function and survive. In what may prove to be the ultimate paradox, you have abundant love available, but are likely not giving it to the person who needs it the most – you. You freely offer it to others, but withhold it from yourself. Why is this so?

Here's an example of how a single incident can be interpreted differently. Suppose I have difficulty speaking in public. I'm scheduled to give a presentation that's required by my job and there's no way I can avoid it. Many of my friends are aware of this and, in fact, attend just to show support. My friends sit in the front row and freely offer words of encouragement, knowing the hours of I've spent trying to overcome my fears. I stand at the side of the room waiting nervously to be introduced. Finally, the program begins and I receive an introduction and welcome from the host, who motions me to walk over to the front of the room. As I'm walking towards the podium, I suddenly trip over the computer power cord on the ground and clumsily fall forward. There's a gasp in the room and I sprawl to the floor. The host rushes to my aid and helps me to my feet asking if I'm OK. Dazed, but unhurt, I stand there in utter confusion.

What are the thoughts of my friends? They will doubtless think the following: "Are you hurt;" "What can I do to help you;" "Let me help you calm down and you'll be fine;" "Let me hold you and comfort you;" "You poor thing, you were so ready to give that speech, and now someone has ruined it for you;" "Who was the irresponsible person who carelessly put the cord on the floor;" "How could a person be so reckless and negligently put a cord on the floor without taping it so no one would trip;" "Take all the time you need, and then give that great speech!" Well, you get the idea – my friends would be totally empathetic, supportive and put the blame on someone else. They'd tell me not to be embarrassed because that was an accident waiting to happen. They'd express words of unconditional love and support and encourage me to "dust myself off" and get up there and give a great speech. They'd forget in an instant and say: "Don't worry, you can do it!"

What are my thoughts? "I'm so embarrassed and humiliated;" "I've been clumsy all my life and now I've ruined it;" "I can't believe I made such a fool of myself in public;" "This proves I'm worthless, just like my family told me when I was little;" "I had nightmares of this happening, and now it's come true;" "Why didn't I walk around the cord, it's all my fault;" "Why wasn't I looking when I was walking;" "I'll be fired and never find another job." Again, you get the idea. I'd be thinking negative words of shame, blame, anger, humiliation and failure. My reaction would be harsh and unforgiving. I'd be twice as hard on myself as anyone else. It'd be brutal and take me years to get over it, with the horror replayed in my mind.

How is it possible that the same event witnessed by the same people can be interpreted so differently? Why will your friends provide an outpouring of love, while you react in disgust and self-blame? Why will your friends forget in an instant, while you'll re-play the incident over in your mind for years on end? Why can't you love yourself, like your friends love you? When it comes to you (my nine-year old daughter calls it your "own self"), why can't you forgive and forget?

My advice: learn to love yourself. Practice self-love and develop the healthy habits of a loving person. You'll achieve self-love when that little voice in your head speaks positive words of encourage-ment and support. When you're not to blame for things that are out of your control. When you say, "Oh, well, I tried my best, but things just didn't work out for me. I'll try harder next time." When your voice speaks the same way to your "own self" as you speak to others. When there's equality of perception and reaction.

Looked at a little differently, have negative thoughts ever helped you to accomplish something important in your life? Will the self-concepts of shame and blame help you to achieve your life goals? No, worry and blame will only drag you down and hold you back. You want to have a great life, don't you? Create and hold on to that positive self-image. Learn the appropriate lessons from your mistakes and then quickly move forward.

Treat yourself like the treasure you are. Be your own best friend. Forgive and forget your foibles of the past. Love your "own self."

LIFE LESSONS:

- There are many little life lessons you need to learn.
- Learn these and you'll have a head start on the competition.
- Work diligently to accelerate your life learning curve.
- Head off to training camp, confident a fabulous life awaits you.
- Learn to:
  o Fail
  o Listen
  o Think Before You Speak
  o Accept Criticism
  o Not Take It Personal
  o Be Patient
  o Do Things Right, Not Fast
  o Stay Cool Under Pressure
  o Say "No"
  o Let Go
  o Live in Balance
  o Obey Your Body
  o Express Your Feelings
  o Apologize
  o Write Notes
  o Tell The Truth
  o Keep Your Word

- o Smile
- o Love Yourself
- Treat yourself like the treasure you are.
- Be your own best friend.

11. ACCOUNTABILITY

There are certain words that carry a higher level of importance. Words that carry deep meaning. Accountability is one of those words. Aspire to be accountable.

Being accountable means being fully engaged and responsible for your actions. It means attaining a higher level of consciousness. At this level of thought, you're aware that your decisions reflect your priorities and you've carefully laid out the options in front of you. You understand your decisions have consequences, and will impact your life in one, three or five years. You've connected the dots and understand that, while there are many choices, only a few will build a great foundation. This means, of course, that to achieve success, you must work hard and sacrifice the pleasures of today for the opportunities of tomorrow. Nothing good can be attained without diligent effort and you're fully prepared for the journey of less in the short run. Greatness, in whatever form, requires sacrifice.

Do you know someone who's fully accountable? What does their life look like? I've been fortunate to have many friends and colleagues who are fully accountable. I look up to them and respect them greatly. I only wish I could be as good as them. While I aspire to be like them, I fall short.

What are the characteristics and habits of someone who lives a life based on accountability? The first thing I notice is how well they take care of themselves. Over the years, they always look healthy and look the same. Their complexion doesn't change and their weight doesn't vary. They have bright eyes and radiate positive energy. This occurs because they take care of themselves.

They eat right, understanding "you are what you eat." When you take them to lunch, they eat the fresh fish of the day and steamed vegetables or baked chicken and salad. They drink lots of water and don't consume soda. You don't see them drink an alcoholic beverage during working hours or on a business flight. They'll enjoy some wine with dinner (like the French), but will drink only in moderation and "after hours." They exercise regularly and have many active hobbies, such as hiking, cycling or golf. They are fit of mind and fit of body.

An accountable person has well-developed limits and bound-aries. They have their priorities and act in a manner consistent with them. They are goal-oriented and goal-focused. This means that if you ask them to do something and they agree, you can count on them to perform. Similarly, they may often say "no," not because what your asking is not worthy (it probably is), but because what you're asking is not within their priorities and abilities to perform. They are highly disciplined and can decline with ease, knowing when they don't have the extra time available. Simply, you can't get them to do something they don't want to do or that's not good for them. They're not easily influenced by outside forces – instead, they're closely attuned to an internal compass with a "True North." They do what's right, not what's popular.

An accountable person lives life with grace and gratitude. They recognize "it's not about them" and wouldn't think other-wise. They're deeply concerned for those less fortunate and are involved in church and charity. Often, they'll do their charitable work anonymously, with little fanfare. It's about helping others, not about getting recognition for something you should be doing anyway.

Are you prepared to live a life of accountability? Will you be accountable and take responsibility for the decisions you make? When you fall short, will you apologize and work extra hard to "make it right?" Will you take care of yourself and live with high standards? Do you have the courage to stand up to the crowd and say "no thanks," when asked to go along? Are you prepared to take the long, lonely path of hard work and sacrifice necessary to reach your goals? Are you capable of "setting the bar high" and then executing on that commitment over a sustained five-year period? Are you ready to be accountable to those you love, your parents, spouse and children and "do right?" Do you have your "True North" compass in place to guide you away from trouble and temptation?

My wish for you is that you embrace the depth and meaning of the word "accountable" and live into it from this day forward. If you do, you'll be better able to handle the tough times and more equipped to reach your full potential as a human being. With accountability as your guide, there's no question you can fulfill your destiny. Without it, well, good luck with that!

LIFE LESSONS:

- Being accountable is important.
- A person with accountability operates at a higher level.
- You're fully engaged in all aspects of life.
- You work hard and sacrifice today for the pleasures of tomorrow.
- You're highly disciplined in your personal and professional life.
- You're respected and respectful, with well-defined limits and boundaries.
- You have a "True North" compass to guide you away from trouble and temptation.
- When you fall short, you take responsibility, apologize, and work extra hard to make it right.
- Being accountable is an ingredient necessary to help you maximize your potential and fulfill your destiny.
- Imagine the kind of person you'd be if you lived a life of accountability.

PART III:
PARADIGMS SHIFT:
PARADOXES APPEAR

12. WHAT MOTIVATES YOU

Have you taken the time to examine your passions and interests in life? What is it that causes you to get fired up? Simply, what motivates you?

There are many possibilities and your life will be greatly improved if you can discover your source of motivation. This is important for at least two reasons. First, it will help you to keep moving forward in a positive direction. Motivation in your life is like fuel in a racecar. You can have a great car, but if you don't have the gas, it won't be worth much or attract much interest. It'll just sit there. Similarly, if you have a great education or training, for example, but don't do anything with it, then you haven't taken full advantage of the opportunities given to you. At each stage of your life, you must be motivated to take on the next challenge and the next step upward. Second, motivations can be a negative factor in your life that must be dealt with and controlled. Any motivation, taken to extremes, can be counterproductive and ultimately harmful if not properly harnessed.

Some are motivated by money, others by power. Some will have mixed motivations, but with fear as an ultimate influence. Many are motivated by an inner competitiveness, a drive for greatness. Others are motivated to "play it safe" and avoid conflict or controversy. A few set out to "right the wrongs" in the world and take on causes that will give them that opportunity. A small number reject the corporate/business world and dedicate their life to humanitarian causes or to church or charity.

With as many possibilities as there are people, it seems, what are the motivators in your life? This is an interesting question, because a person's belief system begins forming in childhood and even common experiences can produce an opposite affect. Two people can grow up in a family without money, and one will be a saver (because she didn't have money) and the other a spender (because he didn't have money). Both lived a childhood without, but formed an opposite system of values. This will also be affected by their birth order and the dynamics of sibling interactions. If the older sister got what little money there was, the middle child might have extreme views about money and might, for example, develop the urge to hoard.

The following exercise has no basis or foundation in research or science. I just made it up. It's a simple exercise to encourage you to uncover the "motivators" in your life. Take out a sheet of paper and write these kinds of descriptive words down: money; food; hunger; sacrifice; competitor; giver; excellence; being first/perfectionist; satisfied; adequate; never enough; people pleaser; get even/retaliation; loved/unloved; creative/artist [add any other words that may apply to you or your childhood]. Then, after writing these words down in random order, go back over your list and circle the words that evoke a strong response. What jumps out at you? What kind of person are you – are you an aggressive competitor, a person who needs excellence in the classroom, a hungry child who lived in fear, or a satisfied child who had a wonderful/loving childhood with everything supplied and never a want or care in the world?

If you're curious, you shouldn't rely on my "made up" list above. Instead, you should read the literature and discover your personality profile. Find the books written by the personality experts, complete with personality profile exercises. These personality tests can help to uncover the things that motivate you and the fears that hold you back. In fact, many employers require a personality profile test as a method to further evaluate your suitability for the job you're being considered for.

Learn about your personality and uncover what motivates you. This exercise in self-discovery will help you stay motivated and encouraged. It will also provide balance by helping you to manage and harness these forces. Finally, when working with others, be mindful that what motivates you, may not necessarily motivate them.

LESSONS LEARNED:

- What motivates you?
- This is an important exercise in self-discovery.
- Some are motivated by money, fear or power.
- Some are natural born leaders, and others want to be led.
- Others pursue history, and humanitarian causes.
- Identify and understand the positive and negative affects these forces/beliefs can have in your life.
- Find jobs/careers that are in tune with your motivations.
- Motivations are unique, and what motivates you, may not motivate others.
- You can be led by your passions, or controlled by your fears.
- How much of your potential do you want to realize? How good do you want to be?

13. COGNITIVE DISSONANCE

Cognitive Dissonance is, generally speaking, the holding of two thoughts or beliefs that are in conflict or opposition. You believe both are true, but you recognize and are troubled by the inherent conflict. It's like being an environmentalist and driving an old black-smoke emitting SUV that gets eight miles to the gallon or working as a fitness director and smoking cigarettes. Over time, the conflict must be resolved. You'll do this by either discarding one of the beliefs and changing to bring your conduct into harmony (stop smoking) or you'll remain unchanged and simply rationalize the differences away (I don't smoke that much, and no one knows anyway).

Throughout your life, you'll be faced with many times in which you are uncomfortable and your thoughts are in seeming conflict. For whatever reason, you won't feel good about the situation and you'll wonder why life is more difficult and the fun has been taken away. Depending on your level of self-awareness, you'll spend time alone thinking things through and begin to identify the issues that are troubling you and why. There will be some particularly difficult times, where you'll need the perspective offered by self-help books, a group at church or a good therapist to uncover your emotional mysteries. You're not alone. You're not the first person in human history to be faced with seemingly intractable problems. The only mistake is waiting and not getting the help you need soon enough. I'll leave the rest to the experts.

I can't help you understand your personal struggles, but I can point out some aspects of life and reality that may help you comprehend the bigger picture. For starters, there's the notion of equality. You need to understand how this evolves as your life evolves. If you don't, life will prove downright confusing.

As kids, we're raised with the notion that things are fair and equal. In the adult world, the reality is nothing could be further from the truth. Things are almost never equal and "fairness" has nothing to do with it. The sooner you can make this transition from child environment to adult reality, the better off you'll be. Understanding that things aren't equal and then comprehending how this plays out in different situations is critical to your future. With this knowledge at hand, it's a matter of adjusting your mindset so that you see things more clearly. Ultimately, your objective should be to see the reality of the situation as it is, not as you want it to be.

In both your business and personal life, the situation is never equal and the stakes are never the same for the two parties involved. It never is and it never will be. Believe otherwise at your peril.

In a business setting, you are either "over" or "under." You have a position that puts you somewhere in a chain of responsibility. You're the boss or the employee, the superior or subordinate. It follows that the person with the higher position, or with a greater level of visibility, will be held to a higher level of accountability and inherently has more to lose. For example, conduct between office interns may be glossed over, but that same conduct between the office manager/supervisor and intern will be cause for dismissal. The person in a supervisory role is held to a "knows better" standard and whatever interpretation is involved, will have a tendency to go against the supervisor. After the chips are counted, you're likely to lose.

It's important to think about this positional inequality and factor it in to your personal code of conduct ahead of time. If you're a talk show host, you can't "lose it" with a caller who's baiting you. If you're a head coach, you can't "go off" on a reporter who's sole objective is to get a story and get noticed. If you're a public official, you can't "yell and scream" at a protestor who's yelling at you. While these may be obvious, I'd submit that the "inequality" analysis applies more frequently than you imagine. Think before you act, and determine who has more to lose. If it's you, don't go there.

Inequality can play out in other ways as well. I had a friend who was extremely loyal to his company and was trying to make every decision in favor of loyalty. I explained that, while loyalty is important and to be valued, it must be factored in to a larger equation. His company has 100 employees, but he has only one job. At some point, his loyalty to his family must outweigh his loyalty to his company. The stakes are not equal. The reality is, you can and must love your company, but your company can't love you back. It's inanimate. The company must make money or it will fail and dissolve. If the recession causes a decline in business and the one-hundred-person workforce must be "right-sized" to eighty, then twenty people must be let go. If he knows that business is down, then he needs to do two things: work harder to be invaluable and start looking for another job "just in case." Isn't this being responsible and proactive with your career? At some point, loyalty has nothing to do with it, and personal responsibility must take over. It's the business of life.

There are other, less obvious, areas of life that are unequal and out of proportion. These will cause you to experience disharmony and discontent – creating periods of cognitive dissonance. For example, disappointments and failures are big. While there's no question you learn more from your failures than you learn from your successes, it's important to keep things in perspective. We have a tendency to carry our disappointments with us too far and too long. Like a baseball pitcher who just threw a home run ball, it's important to have a short memory. Next batter, new pitch, new opportunity to get them out. Always look forward and focus on the next task at hand. Better equipped for the next battle, you should have even more confidence knowing you "won't make the same mistake twice."

While disappointments are big, personal growth and progress towards your life goals are small. Working towards big goals, it's hard to measure progress. Often, it feels like weeks go by with nothing accomplished. On the other hand, if a minor setback occurs, that event seems to take on oversize significance. With disappointments magnified and the small steps of progress largely ignored, it's no wonder we have a tendency to feel bad. The objective is to view our problems/setbacks, on the one hand, and our little successes, on the other, with equal, balanced thought. While things go wrong, you don't have to.

LIFE LESSONS:

- Cognitive Dissonance occurs when you hold two beliefs that are in opposition or conflict.
- Be self-aware and understand the source of internal conflict.
- In any situation, the stakes are never equal.
- Your role/status puts you in a "power over" or "power under."
- Understand the power equation and factor in the inequality.
- If this means you'll lose if you engage in an activity, decide in advance "not to go there."
- You must love your company, but your company can't love you back.
- Ultimately, your loyalty to your family must be factored in.
- Be smart and proactive about your career.
- Build your skills and polish your resume "just in case."
- Learn from and build on your mistakes.
- Like a pitcher, develop a short memory and always look forward.
- With equal balance, recognize and celebrate your successes.
- Progress occurs in little steps.
- A positive attitude will sustain you during the difficult times.
- Never give up. Never give in. It's not an option.

14. ETHICS

No doubt, this is a biggy. However, this book is written in the "less is the new more" format, so this discussion will be brief and to the point. Besides, I'm sure you're already "ethical" and committed to "do the right thing for the right reasons." Here goes.

In my experience, it's not one big ethical violation that will get you in trouble. You don't do everything within the letter of the law with the highest ethical standards, and then suddenly wake up one day and commit a huge ethical violation. Life doesn't work that way.

Ethics is a slippery slope of little things. Seldom do you read about the ethics case involving one big lapse committed in isolation. Rather, it's an accumulation of little discernable ones that, over time, become overwhelming. Initially, there's no cause for concern and the situation seems under control. Then, suddenly, it's too late to turn back. Try as the person may, the scheme/fraud/ violation cannot be unwound. Instantly, it seems, the little things spiral out of control. It's as if they all start small and then grow like a weed. Soon, the garden is gone, leaving a tangled mess.

The message? Ethics matters and the decision to make little ethical lapses, while seemingly innocuous at the time, accumulate into a mess. Decide in advance that you'll take the ethics high road. Not only is it the right thing to do, but there are others watching too. It may be your subordinates or team members, but others will be curious about your character and looking to you to establish the standard of conduct (good or bad). Your character takes years to build, but only moments to destroy, so be vigilant.

There will be times in your life when others question your judgment ("Nothing will happen, you're being ridiculous!"), but stay the ethical course. This will require courage and may be difficult. But a great life requires courage, so get used to it. When I have ethical issues, I don't try to resolve them alone. There's always someone available to help. Seek out others and ask for his or her advice. It may be a trusted supervisor, an ethics officer in your company, or your company's in-house legal counsel. It may be as simple as asking: "What would you do in this situation?"

Ethical conduct is a habit formed early in your career. Start immediately, from Day 1, with high standards. At a minimum, you'll sleep better. According to Mark Twain, there may be an added benefit to consider: "If you tell the truth, you don't have to remember anything."

LIFE LESSONS:

- Do the right things for the right reasons.
- Have a strong moral compass to guide you.
- Ethical decisions are a test of character.
- Character is what you do when no one is looking and you're confident you'll never get caught.
- Decide in advance to take the ethics high road.
- At times this may be difficult and require courage.
- Ethics is a slippery slope of little things.
- Initially, it may be something small.
- "Everybody does it" or "C'mon, get on board."
- "It's not a big deal and nobody will find out."
- Little transgressions will accumulate. Suddenly, it'll be too late to turn back.
- Others will be watching and judging your character.
- Your character takes years to build, but only moments to destroy.
- Mark Twain said: "Always do right. This will gratify some people and astonish the rest."
- Sleep well, my ethical friend!

15. PREPARATION

Your success as a student will be determined by how hard you study. Your success in the "real world" after you graduate will be determined by how hard you prepare. It's a competitive world out there and they're not giving away what you want. You must earn it. Be assured your competitors are doing the extra work necessary to prepare for their success. The only question is, will you be up to the challenge and can you sustain your drive for excellence over an extended period of time? At various times, you'll be tempted to conclude: "I'm smart enough, I've done enough and this is good enough." If you stop short, you may still succeed, but your risk factor goes up. When you least expect it, a lack of preparation will "bite" you. That's the other side of the Free Will equation, isn't it?

Assuming you've made the decision to spend the extra time and effort to prepare, the question is "How do you do it?" What does "preparation" look like and when do you know you've done enough? That's hard to judge and may be determined by your work environment. Look at what others are doing, especially those around you who you respect, and follow their lead. Find the leaders/performers and be more like them. If they get to work early, or spend thirty minutes of their lunch hour working on an article they want to get published in a professional journal, you know they're setting the bar. Ask them for their advice and thoughts on the extra things you could be doing. They'll be happy to oblige.

The more challenging question is how do you do something for the first time? How do you do something, if you've never done it before? How do you get experience, if you don't have any experience?

As a lawyer starting out, I was continually faced with assignments, cases, projects and challenges that were new. It turns out that three years of reading old cases in law books does not prepare you for much of what reality dishes out. Law school prepares you to be a great law student, but not necessarily a great lawyer dealing with the dynamics of the human environment. Imagine that - reality different than the classroom – who would've guessed? I feel like I've been faced with an endless supply of "I've never done that before" experiences. Do you see my underlying problem creeping up again – clueless!

In law school, I was assigned to write my first law review article about a recent case. The challenge seemed impossible, since I hadn't done anything like this before and wasn't an English major. I struggled for weeks without any progress. Failure was within my grasp! In desperation, I pulled out the past volumes of Law Review student articles and read them. I found a few that were simpler in structure and content. Using them as a format, I created an outline for my case discussion. Then, I filled in my discussion of the new case in small, distinct elements. Before I realized it, my first article was complete.

With hesitation and fear, I turned it in to the senior editorial board. Later, I was stunned to learn my article was selected for publication. Was it because of my brilliant and insightful legal analysis? Nope, not a chance. It was because they wanted more articles like the ones they'd published in the past. They wanted more of what they were familiar with. I'd figured out what they wanted, and then delivered. Working back-words, and deconstructing, I put my new material in their "tried and true" format for presentation.

After completing the New York University Graduate Tax Program, I was hired by a wonderful Judge to work as her law clerk for two years. She was a brilliant and experienced jurist, and I was a kid from Nebraska. Feeling insecure in the presence of legal greatness, I was worried about how to start my job. More to the point - how do I avoid getting fired? The process worked like this: she'd assign a new case to you, and your job was to write a "first draft" of the opinion for her review. This required enormous effort, because you had to read through the transcript of the trial proceedings and reams of documents entered into evidence. Then you had to read the legal briefs written by each side and do additional legal research to figure out what the answer should be. Facts + Argument + Law = Decision.

I learned quickly from the other clerks that my Judge had the reputation for substantially re-writing the work of her law clerks. "Tearing it up," might be more accurate. While the clerks did their best and produced excellent work, the Judge had strong views that each opinion bearing her name must be "hers." This process of working hard to produce a draft opinion and then seeing it "dismantled" was a source of frustration. It seemed that neither the clerks nor the Judge could close the gap. Applying common sense (I didn't have much else at my disposal!), I thought this was inefficient and there should be a better way. Maybe it was my pride, my desire not to fail, or both, but I didn't want to see my draft opinions "torn up."

Drawing on my prior experience with the law review article, I decided to find cases my Judge had written in the past few years and read them. As I read, patterns emerged. She had a particular style that was hard to detect at first, but if you thought a little deeper, could figure out. Realizing I had nothing to lose, I created a format for her opinions and then followed it by writing in my new case material. I started like she started and ended like she ended. Miraculously, the Judge didn't change too much of my work product. It seemed that I'd learned quickly to write like my Judge. I didn't write an opinion using my style; I worked very hard to write using hers. I used her format and her language wherever possible.

In later years, she remarked that she thought I was a great legal writer and one of her best clerks. I'd laugh to myself, because my secret was to write like her. I succeeded because I delivered what my customer – the Judge – wanted. My law school methodology of reading the prior cases, deconstructing, and creating a format using this "old" material – worked again!

After beginning as a lawyer and attending legal update seminars, I decided I wanted to speak. How do you speak, if you've never spoken? I started by offering to give a "current events" update at my local bar association. They were always looking for speakers so it was a logical place to begin. In July, I was assigned to speak in October. Panicked, I realized I hadn't done this before. What to do? Understanding that preparation and finding out what others had done before was critical, I developed a plan. I attended each of the next two monthly meetings, even though I wasn't interested in the topic. My purpose was to discover how the program worked, how the speaker presented and the form of their written outline. I didn't want to be unique – I wanted to be "just like them!" After attending the two prior sessions, I was well prepared for my talk. My outline was formatted to look just like theirs and I presented like they did. To my surprise, I received great reviews (Hey, good job, kid!), and a speaking career was borne. My secret? Find how others did it before me, prepare to be like them and then make every effort not to be unique!

To summarize, if you're doing something for the first time, begin by finding out as much as you can from those who've gone before. Someone else may be speaking in months prior, others may have written past articles, or even your customer – my Judge – may have prior writings that give you clues about what to do. Get experience by using the experience of others to your benefit.

Preparation involves not only the substance of your work, but being knowledgeable about the form or forum as well. Begin by following the pack. As you progress in your career, there'll be time to develop your own style. But starting out is no time to be unique. Show up that first time having confidence you're "fitting in" and delivering more of what your audience is familiar with. Follow the "tried and true" and build on your little successes.

LIFE LESSONS:

- Success in the "real world" is determined by how you prepare.

- Your competitors are doing the extra work necessary to prepare. Will you work at least as hard as they do?

- Find other leaders/performers in your line of work, and discover the "extra" things they do to be good. Follow their lead.

- Prepare for each interview and every client interaction. Do a computer search of their background and/or company news and be prepared to discuss. Show them you're focused and motivated.

- Never walk into a meeting unprepared (this will take more time than you imagine).

- How do you do something for the first time? Can you get experience, without any experience?

- Find and deconstruct the prior work done by others.

- If you're writing an article for "them," find "their" prior articles and follow their format.

- Be a detective and do a computer search to find their prior work. Learn the format/example and insert your new material in their familiar form.

- Get experience by using the experience of others as your guide.

- This is no time to be unique. Be safe and do what they did!

16. AGE THIRTY-FIVE

While I haven't done the research, experience tells me that age thirty-five is an important time in your life. A time to stop and reflect on where you've been and where you're going.

Assuming a life expectancy in your seventies, thirty-five is about the halfway point. The halftime of a game is important for the coach and players to discuss, in brutal honesty, what's working and what's not. Remember that game plan you prepared in college? Well, that's out the window and a new plan, based on the harsh realities, must be prepared. Your hopes and dreams must be adjusted based on new realities and the new paradigms of an ever-changing world. This time of re-evaluation is a gift. Use it wisely to your advantage.

It's also important to understand that at about this mid-point your perspective will evolve. Prior to age thirty-five, you're largely self-centered and self-absorbed. Whatever you saw you believed to be true. Moreover, you believed that what you saw and experienced was true not just for you, but for everyone else as well. For example, if you lived in one State for your first twenty-five years, you'd think that was the best State in the Union, with the best people (and best sports teams). However those people acted and whatever they did, you'd accept as the way things are and assume that's the way people act everywhere. While developing your version of "I saw it, it's true," there may be side effects. For example, your belief system may lead you to conclude that in order for you to be right, someone else must be wrong. It's a zero sum game with only one right answer, correct?

The first time you travel abroad, you'll be surprised to learn about different cultures and value systems. You'll no doubt be surprised to be a proud American traveling to a foreign country, only to discover they may not like America. Upon further discussion, you'll discover they distrust America because, for five hundred years, their country has been dominated by the then existing world power. Since America is the current world power, distrust is the order of the day. Their nationalistic interests will be heavily influenced by their history and their perception of respect, and nothing you can do or say will change their mind. Suddenly, your parochial view collides with a dynamic, ever changing worldview.

Prior to age thirty-five you thought it was "all about you." You were a fearless risk taker, because you couldn't comprehend the catastrophic consequences just beyond your sight. After studying all these years, you'd believe you knew it all. Satisfied, and smart enough, you stopped growing and learning. You know what you know and that's all you need to know. Comfortable with your existence, you stopped questioning your own assumptions. You found your comfort zone and did everything necessary to stay in it. You believed the sayings in fortune cookies were nonsense and a waste of time.

After age thirty-five, you ask yourself, incredulous: "What was I thinking" and "Why did I do that?" You begin to think "out of body" and understand you are an infinitely small part of the universe. You understand the more you learn, the less you know. Your search for knowledge becomes deep and perpetual. You start contemplating big issues like the meaning of life and the meaning of your life. You wonder: "What was I put on this Earth to do: Why am I here?" If you're not pursuing your dreams and living a life in pursuit of your passions, your sense of regret will tug at you.

The consequences of your decisions over the past ten years have accumulated and hit you with full force. You look in the mirror and realize you are, indeed, the sum of your decisions. You read and save the fortune cookie messages, understanding they represent a thousand years of wisdom. You regret not following the deep meaning: "Keep true to the dreams of your youth." If only I'd listened sooner!

By the way, if you have children, you'll understand it's "not about you" a little more quickly than the rest of us. All your stuff that was so important before kids suddenly disappears - they either took it or trashed it in the course of playful fun. You'll realize that a clean car was a distant memory, never to occur again. They'll always be stale French Fries under the car seat, in case you get hungry!

LIFE LESSONS:

- Age thirty-five is about halftime of the game of life.

- Hopes and dreams must be readjusted for new realities. A new game plan must be developed.

- Conscious re-evaluation is a gift. Use it wisely.

- Prior to this age, you're largely self-centered and self-absorbed.

- Whatever you see or experience, you believe is universally true.

- You were likely a fearless risk-taker; confident you "knew it all." Ego abounds.

- You found your comfort zone, and will do anything to stay in it.

- You believe the sayings in fortune cookies are nonsense and make no sense.

- After age thirty-five, you begin to think: "What was I thinking," and "Why did I do that?"

- You understand the more you learn, the less you know.

- Knowledge and wisdom prove elusive.

- Pondering the meaning of life, you wonder: "What was I put on this Earth to do?"

- You read and save fortune cookie messages, understanding they represent a thousand years of wisdom.

- Here's one: "Keep true to the dreams of your youth."

- If only I'd listened sooner!

17. RANDOM THOUGHTS

I have random thoughts to offer. They don't deserve a chapter, but they don't deserve to be omitted either. Small ideas that might make a difference in your life. Or not! Undeterred, here goes.

Shameless Acts of Self-Promotion. I was taught to approach professional life with humility. You don't talk about your accomplishments or how good you might be. In the course of representing others, you never threaten anyone in an act of bravado (I've run into a few lawyers who seem to believe this is effective advocacy) and you're never disrespectful. If you're going to do something, you do it, not talk about it. Leave the yapping to others and "do." Perform with excellence. In the track world, if we were running a road race, this would be described as "let your feet do the talking."

However, the other side of the equation is that if you don't talk about your accomplishments, no one else will. I've been on both sides of the annual evaluation table (either giving or receiving an evaluation), and a common refrain is "I didn't know you did that! Why didn't you tell me?" Similarly, if I'm appearing before a client and I'm trying to win their work in a competitive new client proposal opportunity, my job is to differentiate myself, and my firm, from the competition. If I don't "sell" my product – my skill set and documented accomplishments - I'm not doing my job.

While you should be humble, you should also prepare to engage in shameless acts of self-promotion. When called for, you need to be your own best advocate. This means being able to, in a factually accurate manner, describe your accomplishments. You may be uncomfortable with this, but get over it. Especially if you're in the world of delivering professional services, you need to deliver a great sales pitch. Yes, be humble, but as if "on call," be prepared to toot your own horn. If you don't toot it, who will? Besides, what good is a silent horn?

As your own best advocate, be prepared to engage in shameless acts of self-promotion. When asked, you must have a focused sixty-second commercial about you and your company/product/service. If the thought of this makes you uncomfortable, you've got work to do!

Organizational Change. You may find yourself joining an organization that needs to be changed. Your company or non-profit organization may be in a state of difficulty or even dysfunction. There are two challenges: figuring out what the problems are and getting the organization to change in a new direction.

I know little about the details of organizational change, but I do know there's an important perspective that may be overlooked. A dysfunctional organization is perfectly organized and structured to reach the results it produces. If it's dysfunctional, then it's perfectly structured to produce dysfunctional results. It didn't get there by accident – there's a lot of time and effort that went into it. There is "perfection" in wrong-headed thinking that produces wrong-headed results. You may perceive it to be "disorganized," but I submit it's actually perfectly organized – in the wrong direction. This can be true of any organization, any group of individuals, even extending to any personal relationship. If you can "think backwards" and grasp this perspective on "perfection," you can begin to appreciate the depth of your challenge. This realization will prevent you from underestimating the force of inertia and the fact that, from top to bottom, completely new and different policies/procedures/incentives must be put on place. It's like trying to change a bad golf swing – sequenced muscle memory must be eliminated before it can be reprogrammed.

Applying this to relationships, one person told me he does things repeatedly (making the same relationship mistakes) because that's what he knows to do. Stated differently, you will do what you do because that's what you know how to do. It's like intently practicing a bad golf swing – the more you practice without changing the problem, the more ingrained the problem becomes. Will practice alone make the ball suddenly go straight? Unlikely.

How do you get an organization to change and move in a different direction? Especially if it's a group of volunteers in a non-profit environment, how do you get them to agree on a different course of action? Your challenge is to get from me to we. This takes time and patience. You'll see the problem and solution clearly and, if someone would just ask you, you could fix the problem in ten minutes tops. However, you can't tell them directly, because they'll resist and even recoil in the opposite direction.

You must seek to influence and facilitate a new way of thinking. You must change the paradigm. Try these three steps to transformation: (1) build consensus, especially that there's a problem that needs to be fixed. They need to recognize the error of their ways - the old system/program is not producing a great result and can't continue; (2) suggest options for change, using powerful words like "what if" and "imagine." Your goal is to get them to believe it was their idea; (3) when the group process has led them to a solution, congratulate them with the words: "Gee, I wish I'd thought of that!"

You Teach People How to Treat You. This is a big lesson to learn in the working world. It's counter-intuitive, because you're supposed to "get along," "go along" and be a team player. You'd think that everyone at work is on the same team and has the same training/style/standards of conduct. However, you'll discover, with human nature being what it is, that the conduct of others will vary.

Understand that "being a team player" does not equate to being a doormat. You're entitled to respect as a responsible adult human being and, for example, are not there to take the entire blame when the team suffers a setback. You can be a great and valuable employee while commanding and getting personal respect. This means you can and should set personal boundaries and limits beyond which you will not allow others to pass. Unfortunately, you'll be tested for any sign of weakness. If others find they can run over you once, they're sure to try it again. On the other hand, if they discover you have limits and boundaries, they'll have a tendency to back off. Do you see how this works?

You teach people how to treat you. With a high degree of self-respect and self-esteem, set clear personal boundaries and limits beyond which you will not allow others to pass. You hold the key. Paradoxically, you must demonstrate self-respect before you'll receive respect from others. You must first value what you want others to value. You'll be tested both personally and professionally. Get this right early in your career. This knowledge is your power.

If you're negotiating with an adversary, you may find others who try to "bully" to get what they want. They may even threaten to "clean your clock" (to put it mildly). If anyone threatens to do something you know they can't do, then it's only a game. Your success at work will be determined, in part, by how quickly you figure out it's not personal. They don't care about you; they're trying to impose their will to get what they want. Remembering it's only a game is of enormous benefit. If someone threatens you, repeat these words: "Game On!"

Doing Stupid Things. Each week, it seems there's a new revelation about a smart person doing a stupid thing. It may be a politician having an affair with a campaign worker (there's a first!), a corporate insider getting charged with "insider trading," or a financier who orchestrated a massive scheme to fund his lavish lifestyle. There's no shortage of highly educated smart people doing monumentally stupid things. After they get caught, they all seem to utter the same words: "I don't know what I was thinking. I let myself and my family down." Gee, ya think?

I have a new idea to deal with this age-old problem. What if, before you decided to do something stupid, you'd call your friend, the lawyer in the Midwest, and ask: "Is it OK if I do [insert stupid thing here]? In real life, the questions would go like this: "I've worked hard to be elected the governor of the State of _____," and I'd like to cheat on my wife/husband with a campaign worker. Is that OK?" "I'm a financial advisor and I have other people's money in my trust account at the bank. Is it OK if I steal it and buy a mansion?" You may laugh, but I'd bet this would cut white-collar crime in half and, when you consider the amount defalcated each year, plus the cost of a criminal investigation, trial and incarceration, my idea could save society hundreds of millions of dollars. I'm sure a new hot line could be established with lawyers on call: 1-800-STUPIDS.

The Art of Selling: Make Them Thirsty. Selling your product or services is all about the customer. You must determine what the customer needs, when the customer needs it, and what price the customer's willing to pay. It's not about your need to sell. It's about making the customer, and his/her business, more successful. Focus relentlessly on your customer and do everything in your power to make them successful. If you can ignore your own wants and needs, and instead "think like your customer," you'll be ahead of the game.

Early in his career, Dad's jewelry store was located in a large department store. With the other employees, Dad would attend a monthly sales meeting designed to keep the sales force focused and motivated. At one such meeting, the owner of the department store was urging the employees to "sell, sell, and sell!" Unconvinced those tactics would work, one skeptical employee raised his hand and said: "Excuse me, Sir. Isn't it true that you can lead a horse to water, but you can't make 'em drink?" Without missing a beat, the wise owner responded: "Yes, it's true that you can't make them drink, but you're missing the point. As a salesman, your job is not to make them drink. Your job, Sir, is to make them *thirsty!*"

How To Find a Dentist (and other professionals). I moved a number of times from one big city to another. With each move, came the necessity of finding a new dentist and doctor. I was frustrated, because how do you find a new dentist who is, in fact, really good? When they all appear equal and you have no basis to judge whether one dentist is actually a better dentist than the rest, what do you do? If you ask them or their staff directly if they're any good, they'll say: "I'm the best!" If you ask a patient, even they'll tend to repeat the mantra – because they're just repeating what they've heard, without the ability to make an independent factual evaluation.

Then it dawned on me. Dentists can't drill on their own teeth! A dentist needs a dentist! Eureka! Since knowledge is power, I decided to try out my dentist-finding system. I walked up to my then neighbor, a dentist, and I inquired: "I'm sure you're a great dentist, but you're a friend and I really don't want to start a professional relationship based on friendship alone. Would you be kind enough to give me the names of two really good dentists?" He said: "Of course." I then talked to those two dentists and asked them: "If you needed dental work, who's the dentist that you'd go to for your dental work?" Out of the three names they mentioned, one name matched. I then went to the finalist and said: "I understand you are actively teaching at professional dental seminars and are a leader in your field. Is this true?" He was so excited, he showed me his lab and demonstrated how proud he was of his attention to detail. I've had this same dentist for nineteen years and he's remarkable. I used this same methodology and found my personal physician. I've been his patient for seventeen years and he's now a favorite of professional athletes. I joke: "I found you first!" and he nods in agreement.

When searching for a new professional, whether dentist, doctor, lawyer or accountant, you need to do your homework. While referrals from others are a start, they're not the end. The goal is to find a person who actually is qualified to know the difference in quality and then ask for their professional judgment. For example, if you ask me to give you the names of two terrific tax lawyers in town, I'll provide them. I can assure you, based on my in-depth experience, they'll be well qualified to handle your matter. So, find the best professional you can on your own, and then ask the professional to recommend two or three others. At that point, you can feel confident the "others" will be well qualified.

A few years ago, I told my dentist about my dentist-finding secret. He laughed in agreement and said that if you really want to find a good dentist, talk to the professionals at the dental labs. That is the intersection of most dentists, and they're the ones who actually see the work product and can provide an objective evaluation. I then asked: "So, who's your dentist in Phoenix?" His answer surprised me: "I get on a plane and fly to San Diego to see a world-famous dentist. He's the only one I trust implicitly." I then said: "So, my system works?" He replied: "Absolutely!"

You'll Be Known By The Friends You Keep. There are many sayings that carry deep meaning. "A person is known by their friends" may be at the top of the list. Your friends speak volumes about you and your character. In order to have great friends, you must first be the friend you hope to find. Being a friend takes time and effort, two things that, over your life, are in increasingly short supply. Friendship speaks of your interests, priorities and connectedness. It's about being selfless and being unconditionally there for someone else. It's about seeing someone at his/her worst and not judging (the joke is that a friend is someone who knows all the bad stuff about you and likes you anyway!).

Stay connected with your friends from the various stages of your life. You'll be amazed at what they grow up to be and what they do. Make new friends in your chosen field. Call them for advice. Build a network of "smarter than you" colleagues. Be attracted to friends who are more accomplished and have higher goals. Even if you "underwhelm" by comparison, your career will be elevated to a higher level just by being in the same room. Surround yourself with people who inspire you. It'll be enormously motivating.

Dogs Look Like Their Owners. I don't know whether owners subconsciously pick dogs that have similarities or whether, over time, dogs and owners meld together and look more alike, but I have this theory that dogs look like their owners. I haven't done the research and I don't have any data to support my theory, but just when I start to have doubts, I see a master walking a dog and am struck by their similarities. It might be the way they walk together, the man's silver beard (he's walking a Scottish Terrier) or the woman's bows that seemingly match (she's walking a Toy Poodle or Yorkie), but I can always find some shared similarity. I may be wrong and I might be imagining things, but I keep discovering new ways masters and their dogs look alike.

Next time you see a master walking his/her dog down the street on a leash, take some time to study, compare and contrast. I'd be curious to know if you notice similarities like I do. Let me know the results of your research!

Laugh. I've intentionally saved the best for last. Imagine how great your life would be if you could laugh. You can't control what happens to you, only how you react. Your reaction is your choice and your decision. What if you could laugh not only with others, but also at the things that happen in your life? What if most of life is not that serious? What if you decided it was a priority to laugh with your loved ones, especially your children? What if you could teach your children to laugh at the crazy things that happen in life (wait, they're kids – they already know how to do that – and should be encouraged!)?

Imagine the kind of person you'd be if your heart were filled with the spirit of laughter. What if your first reaction was to laugh?

LIFE LESSONS:

- Be your own best advocate.
- If someone asks what you do, have a sixty-second commercial about you and your company/product/service.
- Engage in shameless acts of self-promotion.
- Organizations (and relationships) are perfectly organized to reach the results produced.
- To change others, you must seek to influence and facilitate a new way of thinking. Change the paradigm.
- They must believe it was their idea. You should say: "Gee, I wish I'd thought of that!"
- You teach people how to treat you.
- Establish personal boundaries and limits beyond which you'll not allow others to pass.
- Don't give others your emotional "key" without your permission.
- Call a friend before you do a stupid thing.
- A salesman's job is to make the customer thirsty.
- When searching for a new professional, find a person who's actually qualified to know the difference in quality and ask them for recommendations.
- A person is known by their friends.
- Dogs look like their owners.
- Have a heart filled with laughter.
- Imagine if your first reaction was to laugh.

18. THE MEANING OF LIFE

A book on life lessons would not be complete without a discussion about the meaning of life. There are big issues to ponder and what bigger than the true meaning of life. This is one of those philosophical discussions that's been explored and debated for thousands of years. Since this book commits that "less is the new more," it wouldn't be appropriate to identify the various theories and try to either explain or reconcile them. I'll leave that to the deep thinking philosophers and experts – and if you're truly curious, you should research and evaluate on your own. Nope, I plan to explain my simplistic version in the "less is more" format you're now familiar with. Ready?

My theory of life is that all you get is a day. God promises to give you one sunrise at a time and then delivers. Since you have Free Will, what you do with your gift of this day is up to you.

At one extreme, you can start your day stressed and overwhelmed and be negative to everyone you come into contact with. You can complain and act like a victim. You can rush through your day dazed and confused and plop into bed at night exhausted and weary.

At the other extreme, you can start your day with prayer and meditation for the gift of life. You can be thankful for all the gifts and blessings God has bestowed on you. There are so many you can't count. In an attitude of grace and gratitude, you will be calm and positive to everyone you come into contact with. You'll act like a victor, not a victim, and greet others with a smile. The events, activities and demands of the day may be many, but you somehow feel equipped to handle them. You touch base with friends and family. At night, you crawl into your warm bed with a warm heart. Having given your best, you're ready for restful sleep and renewal. You express thanks for the gift of the day just given, and look forward to the gift of the day to follow. You close your eyes in peace.

That's all there is to life. Whether you're rich or poor, healthy or sick, live in a city or on a farm, God gives you the gift of a day. Each day, each gift, begins with a magnificent sunrise. What, you didn't see it this morning? You didn't get up and hike to the top of a hill? You weren't out walking with your spouse, child or pet? You didn't stop to marvel at the magnificence of nature? God places the gifts on your road. If you don't see them and stop to open, that's your issue. You have Free Will and can ignore and rush by – but that doesn't mean they're not there.

What have I missed? You get a sunrise and a day to do with as you please. How you act and the decisions you make are yours. Yes, I'm sorry to say, bad things happen to good people, and there's a lot of trauma and drama, but it's contained in this one day. Tomorrow is a new day, a new start, a new beginning. You can make new decisions tomorrow. You can start on a new path. It may be long, lonely and difficult, but you can do it. If your problems are severe, you can find an expert to help. No matter how difficult, this day and the breaths you take are a gift. Even when it seems unbearable, you'll have the strength to complete it. Even during the dark times of life, when the yolk seems too heavy and your burdens too great, you're not alone. The hope of the next day being a little better will sustain you.

I recently attended a funeral of a contemporary. His family urged those in attendance to celebrate his life, not mourn it. He died of a long bout with cancer. His widow provided a glimpse of his final months. She described in detail what they did together each morning. What time he got up, how he started the coffee maker, let the dogs out and got the paper. How he'd let her sleep in later and bring a mug of coffee to her bedside. How they'd go for a walk and witness the miracle of each sunrise. The description of their life together was so remarkable, so touching, so poignant. Life wasn't about the big things he'd accomplished or the far-away places he'd traveled. No, it was about the joy of their morning routine together. A day in the life; lived in little increments. Turns out, it's the small things that matter.

There it is - the meaning of life. You get a day. Subtracting sleepy time, you get about fifteen hours. That's it. Life's served up in little daily increments for you to make the most of.

As you get older, the days go by faster and life whizzes by in a blur. The other day, I heard a person exclaim: "I can't believe it's almost Thanksgiving: I feel like I just got my taxes done!" I felt the same way. When my children were very young, other parents would say: "I wish mine were like that again. They grow up so fast – you'd better enjoy it – because they'll be gone before you know it!" A parent struggling with little ones is so sleep deprived that she/he can only hope they'd get bigger so you can sleep! However, I heard that comment from so many other parents, I thought it must be true. Sure enough, as my kids get older and begin their teen years, they were right - the time did pass quickly. Having been made aware, and learning this lesson early, I'm doing my best to slow the days down and enjoy the little moments. My immediate goal is to buy more toys and play with them longer.

Last weekend, my nine-year-old daughter was excited to get new shoes. The next morning, she looked at me with a sly smile and said "I was so excited about my shoes, I slept in them!" As we both looked down at her feet, there they were! For the next two evenings, she asked if she could sleep in her shoes again. I said: "Of course!" Wouldn't life be great if you were so excited, you were sleeping in your new shoes? We have much to learn from our children. I'm convinced being child-like can be a virtue.

LIFE LESSONS:

- The meaning of life has been pondered for thousands of years.
- My theory is all you get is a day.
- God promises to give you one sunrise, and then delivers.
- What you do with your gift is up to you.
- You can spend it stressed, overwhelmed and negative. You can live it as a victim.
- At the other extreme, you can start your gift with prayer and meditation, expressing profound thanks for your gift.
- In an attitude of grace, be a victor, not a victim.
- The events, activities and demands will be many, but you'll feel equipped to handle them.
- Tomorrow is a new day, a new start, a new beginning.
- Life is lived a day at a time, in little increments.
- My nine-year-old daughter got new sneakers and she was so excited she slept in them.
- Wouldn't your life be better if you slept in your new shoes?
- We have much to learn from our children.
- I'm convinced being "child-like" is a virtue.

PART IV:
FOUR WORDS

19. FOUR WORDS FOR YOUR JOURNEY

In my prior book, **Things I Wish I Knew – A Compendium of Lessons Learned Late,** I wrote about four words that you'll need for the journey. Any story about "Life Lessons" is not complete without a discussion of four words that will have a profound impact on your life. If you haven't read about these four words, you need to. If you have, the discussion is so important, it bears repeating.

Faith. The first word you'll need for your journey is faith. My faith in God is strong, resolute and unshakable. I've endured tough and lonely times, but I've never been alone. I've felt the heartache of love lost, but I've never felt unloved. I've looked at the mountain of life from the bottom when the view was shrouded, the task seemingly impossible. Then I awakened and realized that with God all things are possible.

I was childless through my thirties, but somehow believed God would provide me with children in His time. I've surrendered my life to Him and I've discovered a depth of peace and love unimaginable. I try to give Him thanks for my many blessings and rely on His Strength during the tough times. I can't do it on my own. The burden's too great. My prayer each day is a simple one I've made up: "Dear God, give me the strength and wisdom to act in your light and love." I'm sure you've made up your prayer and you have your own stories of faith tested and faith applied.

I've always had my faith and have always felt God's guiding hand on my shoulder. However, I spent many years without understanding and truly believing. I thought I was in charge and in control. I felt bad, and took it personally, when things went wrong. I thought I was responsible for the feelings/misgivings/pain of others. I thought I had to carry my burdens alone. Those burdens were beyond me and wore me down. My life was not reaching it's spiritual potential and the burdens too heavy. I could go on, but you know the story from your own life.

For some, it might be difficult to comprehend why faith is important and how different your life will be with it. Imagine you are a sleek, white sailboat. The whiteness is startling to behold and obviously represents the inherent purity of your soul. Your sailboat is sturdy and buoyant, made to withstand the rough seas of life. It has no engine, but relies only on the God-supplied winds to travel on life's journeys. The problem is, Earth consists of endless seas with powerful currents. One moment your boat is heading East in calm waters, and then the winds shift and storms engulf you. Apart from panic, what will you do?

In my imagery, your faith guides your sailboat to the most beautiful cove (probably a computer screen saver picture of Bora Bora). But it's not enough to be in the cove. There's more. You must be tethered to the ocean floor. Your faith in God connects you to Him. If you live in faith, you'll float and move (representing free will), but never stray too far (living true to God's Word). Without fully comprehending, you know you're anchored and made secure by God. What if you don't have faith? Your boat won't be tied down and will blow with the winds. It will be subject to every force, be constantly blown out to sea and tossed around by the vast forces of nature. You'll live a life exhausted at the burdens, responsibilities and uncertainties. You'll have the feeling of being constantly "blown off course." During these times, you'll feel frightened and alone with no one to turn to.

Even with faith embraced, we're a culture in search of knowledge outside of God's realm. I believe our search for "external" help is misplaced. What if you're turning outward, instead of inward, and looking for help in the wrong places? What if God has already given you everything you need? What if you're already equipped for the journey? What if, much like a parent packing a child's back-pack, God has packed yours? What if every answer, every need, is already there for you? What if it's all there if only you'd ask?

Get started and embrace your faith with passion. Spend your life basking in the warmth, glory and grace of God's love. Peace be with you.

Gratitude. Imagine a life filled with gratitude. What would that look like? Your first thought in the morning would be to give thanks for the new day. You'd be humbled at the sunrise and sound of birds chirping. No matter the struggles and difficulties, you'd be thankful for the blessings in your life.

You'd spend a little extra time giving thanks for the blessings, because there are many. You have a roof over your head and food on the table. You have your family and your friends. Your ego would be small. Your sense of grace and gratitude for all you've been giv-en and for this moment in time would be large and overwhelming. Your heart and spirit would be large as well, exuding a loving con-fidence. The people you meet would be lucky to cross your path, because you'd say "Hi" and greet them with a smile. While facing the inevitable challenges of the day, you'd stay true to your beliefs and not be swayed by the emotions of the moment. No one could do anything to you, because you wouldn't allow it. You'd see things clearly as they are and not as you want them to be. You'd have no sense of entitlement, because you're grateful for what you have. You wouldn't pursue objects or be jealous, because you're con-tent with who you are and what you have. Over time, you'd want less, not more. You'd contribute anonymously to charity because of your need to give, not their need to receive. You'd give freely to others "because they need it more than you do."

What does a life of gratitude look like to you? Can you imag-ine living your life with a "gratitude-first" heart? Such a life would provide daily riches and rewards beyond your dreams. Live life "in gratitude."

Courage. If life were easy, we'd automatically make all the right choices. Our decisions, and the consequences that inevitably follow, would fall perfectly in place. The road would be smooth and our future would be predictably wonderful.

However, experience (and country and western song titles) tells us life doesn't work that way. We're faced with choices and decisions that are unclear and difficult. Although we have a "True North" gut instinct to help guide us, we don't often follow it. Why? Because following your gut requires you to do things you don't want to do or face facts you don't want to face. Following your gut requires you to take the long, painful road and delay instant gratification. Making tough decisions requires you to do what you don't want to do, at a time when you don't want to do it. It's like driving through the fast food window and ordering vegetables and vitamin water. These good decisions often require that you not follow the crowd. When your so-called friends are waiving you down the wrong path, you must waive "goodbye" and take the other, lonely, fork in the road.

Making good decisions and following your gut requires something that's in short supply. Courage. Yes, it takes courage to walk away and choose the lonely path required of a great life. It takes courage to say "no" to your so-called friends. It takes courage to say "no" to a relationship that's not good for you. It takes courage to seek help and overcome your own problems. It takes courage to change. It takes courage to lead an authentic life with an authentic voice. When you have children, it takes courage to tell them: "I don't care what your friends have or what their parents let them do. Our family has our own set of rules and our own unique way of doing things and we're not going to change just because someone else is doing it." It takes courage give your children loving discipline, instead of being a friend who says, "yes" all the time.

I hope you grab an extra helping of courage. It's free and available to anyone. I hope you call your true friends (there's only a few) and ask them for their help and support in order to gain more courage. I hope you lead an authentic life with an authentic voice built on courage.

Forgiveness. Of all the words, forgiveness may present the greatest challenge. It's something we need to both give and receive.

On the giving side, have you forgiven someone lately? If so, did you find it easy to forgive or was it difficult? Did you quickly forgive someone after "being wronged" or did it take you a long period of time? While forgiving someone is good for them, it is far more important for you to do the forgiving. Why? Until you've forgiven someone who's hurt you, you'll remain locked in the emotional chains of the past. You'll remain an emotional prisoner and carry the memory with you everywhere. Simply, it's the last act you need to perform to "get over it once and for all." Please, do yourself an enormous favor and forgive someone. Forgiveness of others will free your spirit and allow you to move forward with your wonderful life. Forgive them because they deserve it? Not necessarily. Forgive them because you deserve it more.

On the asking side, for whatever reason, it's not easy to ask for forgiveness. The more we need to be forgiven, the harder it is to ask. Especially when we do something that hurts a loved one, it seems our ego is in the way. Our own weaknesses prevent us from doing the right thing and the best thing: asking for forgiveness. If you want to live a life of accountability, and bring your loved ones closer, learn to say "I'm sorry" and "I apologize." Then follow those words with "Will you forgive me?" These words are especially powerful when you say them to your children. You are modeling an important behavior they need to learn and showing your children enormous respect. Watch their expressions and attitudes change and bring them closer.

If you're good at taking responsibility for your actions and apologizing, if you're good at asking for forgiveness, your friends and loved ones will be lucky indeed. If you're also quick to forgive others, your life will be truly blessed. What are you waiting for? There's someone in your life at this moment that you need to forgive. Forgive them because you deserve it more. Oh, and by the way, the person that may need forgiving may be you. So, give yourself the ultimate gift. Forgive yourself and you'll be rewarded with a truly extraordinary life filled with love and joy. Do it today!

PART V: CONCLUSION

I wish life came with an instruction manual. My life didn't, and my life's journey was made more difficult. I was unprepared for the complexities of life and the complexities of the workplace. I learned most of my lessons late and the hard way. I needed wise thoughts and a periodic correction to keep me in line and focused on the road ahead. I needed someone to tell me what I didn't want to hear when I didn't want to hear it. I needed a coach yelling in my ear: "Stay focused. Keep your head down. Execute your assignment!" I needed a "life manual" – my personal playbook - tucked in my drawer so I could pull it out in my time of need. Yes, my life would've been made better if I had some pointed directions on how to "trouble shoot" my way out of trouble. Granted, I wouldn't have been spared the difficulties I've experienced, but I would've been better equipped to understand and deal with them.

Your life can be better. With guidance and wisdom, you can accelerate your learning curve on your way to maximizing your potential. In fact, my wish for you is that the treasures of the rainbow will be yours. However, they're not giving away what you want. You must work hard and be prepared to sacrifice to reach your goals. Are you interested? Are you ready to take on the challenges on your road to success? I know you can do it. Let's get started.

Learning the lessons of Icarus, you're grateful for your gifts and will live modestly, with your ego in check. You'll do your best to live with humility as your guidepost and listening to and respecting others. When you need help "coming back to earth," you'll have friends and family there to support you. Heeding the investment advice of Mr. Buffett, you'll be focused on a great education. It might be a four-year college, or a great community college or technical school, but you'll get a degree so you have "something they can't take away from you." Never satisfied, you'll pursue life with the passion of a life-long learner.

As if designing a home, you'll have carefully considered your options and developed a career plan that is robust and aggressive, yet realistic. It'll be "stress-tested" by others who know you well and approved. Life goals in place, and an education to support your ambitions, you'll be off to a great start. You'll stop dreaming and start doing, understanding that your goals will ignite your power of intention. With persistence in your back pocket, you fully appreciate that anything worth having must be earned through hard work, sacrifice and diligence. You're prepared for the inevitable setbacks and you're even ready to use adversity to your best advantage.

You understand the importance of good decision-making and understand your decisions add up to the "you," you're looking at in the mirror. So far, you like who you see in the mirror and want no part of any decisions that detract from the great person you are. Your courage and faith has been, and will be, tested. You know the "right" path is often the most difficult and lonely one. Undeterred, you move forward and live life looking through the windshield and not the rear-view mirror. You've learned worry is not a helpful energy. Besides, nothing you've worried about has come true.

Your generation will be faced with an extraordinary pace of change, but you're adaptable. You've lived with change all your life and are ready to use your imagination and develop a vision for your future. Although human nature never disappoints, you still have faith in others and believe your career/business will be more successful if it's about people, not money. You have mentors from each stage of your life, and keep in touch with some great teachers and a favorite coach. Already, you've been sought out for advice by others, and are being asked to mentor others.

You've had to learn some lessons, a few the hard way. Listening is a challenge, patience is "for the birds," and failure is tough. You take it personally, but that's because you care and are passionate. Saying "no" and letting go are hard tasks. You're improving at expressing your feelings and feel empowered when you're your own best advocate. Smiling comes naturally, but loving your "own self" may be the most difficult of all. Is this where "patience" comes back in?

You have great friends and are a great friend in return. You're always there for others and your voice is soothing. You have bright eyes and radiate positive energy. Accountability is proving difficult, but that's because the bar is set high. Your motivations are mixed, causing constant confusion. You want to be led by your passions, and not controlled by your fears. Easier said than done.

It hasn't been easy and the challenges seem large. You've had to reevaluate and readjust your life goals based on changing conditions, but you're still "on track." Recently, you've started saving the fortune cookie sayings, placing them in a little box. The wisdom of a thousand years touches your soul. Using the "secret system," you've found a great dentist and doctor and you've become fast friends. After your annual check-ups, you send your familiar hand-written notes telling them how much their skillful care is appreciated. You never believed it, but you've recently noticed dogs look like their master. You thought that theory was "crazy," but you find yourself questioning your own judgment. "Maybe dogs and people just meld together over time, like old married couples do," you rationalize.

You couldn't have made it without your four words. Faith is first and most important. It's your bedrock and you're moored safely in God's lagoon. You've made up your own simple prayer and have many stories about your faith tested and faith applied. You've been alone, but never felt alone – God's comforting hand is always on your shoulder. Your sense of grace and gratitude are profound and you freely give to others because they need it more than you do. At times, your courage has been in short supply. A lack of courage has caused you to take little steps down the wrong path. You now fully appreciate that a great life requires you to make tough decisions – doing what you don't want to do, at a time when you don't want to do it. "Oh well, life ain't easy," you say to no one in particular. Forgiveness has proven a daily challenge. It's not easy to give, and even harder to receive. Yep, still working on that one!

Here's the Grand Finale: You are made in God's image. Honor God's creation and love yourself as God loves you. There will be dark days, but fear, doubt and darkness exist only with your permission. Walk in the way of lightness and love. Be the best authentic you. Find the fun and laugh. If you love and laugh, I'm confident the treasures of the rainbow will indeed be yours.

ENDNOTES

PART I

Metamorphoses (Kline) 8 The Ovid Collection, University of Virginia E-Text Center, Book VIII: 183-235 Daedalus and Icarus.

"Warren Buffett Featured in University of Nebraska Ad Campaign," GoodNUz, p. 28 (Fall 2008).

The quotes from my father and other phrases used are commonly attributed to such notables as Confucius, Lao Tzu, Ben Franklin, Vince Lombardi, Mark Twain, Thomas Keating and Yogi Berra.

PART II

Kevin Leman, The Birth Order Book (Grand Rapids: Revell 1998)

From the film Star Wars, Episode V – The Empire Strikes Back: 20th Century Fox, 1980

PART III

Wikipedia (Definition of "Cognitive Dissonance")

Larry Bossidy and Ram Charan, Execution: The Discipline of Getting Things Done (New York: Crown Publishing Group 2002)

Malcolm Gladwell, Outliers: The Story of Success (New York: Little, Brown and Company 2008)

Christopher Buckley, "What Were They Thinking?," The Wall Street Journal W3, March 6-7, 2010

ACKNOWLEDGEMENTS

A great life in general, and a book in particular, requires a strong supporting cast. Many times in life, you don't think of things or do things on your own. It takes others who believe in your greater capabilities to get you motivated towards higher goals. It takes others on the sidelines urging you to "get in the game" because "you can do it." But for the belief and encouragement of others, my career would've taken a dramatically different direction, and this book would've never existed. Yes, others do make a difference in your life.

I'd like to thank my long-time assistant, Sherry Ledington, for encouraging me to write this book. She believed I had talent (a small amount, to be sure) to write "not" like a lawyer. She saw my ability to take the complexity of the tax law and reduce it to words and concepts clients could understand and she openly wondered why I couldn't do that with the complexity of life. With that challenge in mind, I started an outline, then the Preface. So a book was borne.

A book about "Life Lessons" can only be written because of the many who contributed to my career. It began in high school with my teachers, Stephanie Lonnquist, Wally McNaught and Frank Solich. I had a great liberal arts education at Nebraska Wesleyan University and met, and introduced, Carol Mozak and Paul Wolff (who later married). In law school, two professors, Dave Ludtke and John Gradwahl, gave me the "tough love" I needed and taught me how to write better and with fewer words. Adrian Fiala gave me my first job in Nebraska as a lawyer and I'm forever appreciative of his friendship. Leaving Nebraska, I attended the New York

University Graduate Tax Program where I formed friendships with my classmates and professors alike (adversity (survival?) adds a special bond, so I learned.).

The Honorable Irene F. Scott (deceased) gave me the privilege of serving as her law clerk and taught me lessons I could only understand later in life. She made me a better person before making me a better lawyer. While at the Tax Court, I made many lasting friendships with the other clerks, including a special one with Professor Howard Abrams, Emory Law School. He's my designated "phone a friend," should I ever appear on a game show ("The final category is mathematical physics to win the game." Howard, where are you – answer the phone!).

I received my first case assignment as a lawyer from David Elrod. The case was impossible, but he refused to let me give up or give in. "Losing" is not in his vocabulary. He showed faith in my abilities when I thought I had none and taught me to "get tough" when I needed it most. We worked together on that case for three years and that experience should be the subject of another book (and movie soon to follow). He's given me countless doses of wisdom for the ages.

There are too many other lawyer friends to mention who've helped me and I'm indebted to them all. My friends in the bar association and colleagues in my accounting firm and email discuss group have made me a better lawyer and, at times, literally helped me to survive in the profession. "Nowhere" begins to describe where I'd be without them. To this day, I'm grateful they laugh at my song titles. My mentors and friends, Scott Bloom, Paul and Carol Wolff, David Ludtke, Howard Abrams, Stef Tucker, Milt Hyman, Lou Weller, Jeff DeBoer, David Weiss, Charlie Pulaski, Steve Renna, Rick Carlson, Dan Tucker and Charlie Siddle have seen me through the best and worst of times. Some still like me!

My golf instructor, Mike LaBauve, should be coaching me about life instead of teaching me about golf (an impossible task to date). My golf fitness trainer, Steve Heller, motivates me to burn one more calorie by doing something I don't want to do. My friends at the Wharton School of Business, especially Kathy Pearson and David Wessels, inspired me to think in new ways about the business of life.

Portions of this book were inspired by the teachings of Pastor Kelly Bender and staff at the Paradise Valley United Methodist Church.

Finally, my sister Sharon taught me how to bake an apple pie and always believed in me even when my actions proved her wrong. When I'd call her, exasperated, for child-rearing advice, she'd repeat: "Freddy, you are smarter than a two-year-old!" Words to aspire to.

ABOUT THE AUTHOR

Fred received a B.S. in Business Administration from Nebraska Wesleyan University; a J.D. from the University of Nebraska College of Law; and an LL.M. in Taxation from New York University. He served as an Attorney Advisor for the Hon. Irene F. Scott, United States Tax Court in Washington, D.C. Fred works for a national accounting firm in Phoenix, Arizona.

In 2007, the International Who's Who of Business Lawyers named him to Who's Who Legal. In 2008, he was named an outstanding alumnus in the field of law by Lincoln Southeast High School and recognized as a Master by the University of Nebraska Lincoln. Fred was featured in an article on golf fitness in **The New York Times** and has appeared in an infomercial with Mike LaBauve on **The Golf Channel**.

Fred is the author of **Things I Wish I Knew: A Compendium of Lessons Learned Late** (Booksurge 2009). He's a divorced dad with three amazing gifts, Aaron (15), Tyler (13) and Olivia (9).

For more information, visit: www.fredwitt.com

18125215R00083

Made in the USA
Charleston, SC
17 March 2013